Copywriting Essentials For Content Marketing

TABLE OF CONTENTS

Author's Note

Thank you for investing your time and energy in reading this book.

It contains steps to help you write better ad and content copy; however, its primary goal is to give you a sound understanding of why some content converts at a much higher rate than others.

I intend to teach you how to write copy that holds readers on your website longer or entices them to click to a destination of your choice.

It has nothing to do with how long or pretty your text & formatting is. Instead, it has everything to do with who your audience is, how well you understand a reader's motivations for wanting to buy, the reasons why they might not buy, and how to effectively weave these motivating factors into your content.

You may have noticed I used the word energy and not money in the opening paragraph of this book. That's because, if you think about it, money is just crystallized energy. When you write, you have the opportunity to effectively turn your time and energy into profit through compelling content.

How much value you deliver to your audience, how much you can relate to your reader, and how much you help them will determine how well you will earn their trust and business. The difference between average writers and outstanding writers is apparent in their practice of this philosophy throughout their content.

I've studied the world's most successful authors and copywriters. I've even been lucky enough to have been mentored by some. If you learn from these personalities, they all follow similar principles and patterns.

They create content that addresses specific human needs,

wants, and desires. They do this by building a rapport with readers and are, therefore, preconditioning them to want to buy.

I've been writing since I was eight years old. As a child, while travelling with my family for 1 year, I had to write letters home as part of my homework. I had to write a 5-page letter every second day. I learned how to be creative and engage with the recipient of the message, and tell a story, so they didn't become bored with the constant barrage of letters I was sending them. I caught the writing bug - and that early experience taught me how to get creative when there seemed to be nothing to write about!

Later in life, my interest in writing carried through to the study of commercial ad and marketing copy. What I found was that the framework traditional marketing taught was all focused on ME ME ME marketing and was not customer-centric. School teaches us to write copy that is categorized and separated into specific informational, storytelling, business or creative genres, then grammatically corrected and 'professionally' formatted - Joe Average training.

The average conversion rate for the most widely taught styles of writing is generally between 1 and 3 percent. Not very exciting. In hindsight, it's obvious why there is such a massive variance in conversion rates between writers, and a 1 to 3 percent conversion rate is a far cry from the 20 plus percent some top copywriters' articles can generate.

In 2003 I began a career as an internet marketer. The rule was that I must spend thousands of hours writing then posting as many articles and other content I could to build traffic to my websites. As you can imagine, if I was aiming for a conversion rate of 1 to 3%, I had to write a LOT of content, which seemed like an overwhelming task to complete in a short space of time. I felt inauthentic after a while writing what I now call "quickie" content because the whole process was all about producing a large quantity of hastily written low-value articles rather than a small number of quality articles with impressive conversion rates.

By 2007 I had built several websites, but I very quickly reached burnout out with the number of hours I had to spend on topics that were supposed to be fun, but turned out to be a significant pain in you know what!

I had all but given up on the vision widely touted by "guru's" about earning "passive income online." This goal seemed harder and harder to achieve. I still loved the concept of writing for a living but disliked the poorly targeted, inefficient content marketing strategies taught everywhere online. So I invested in what turned out to be a game-changing course, a $17000 investment (many principles in that course you will learn in this book), and read every book I could find by the world's top copywriters.

Of all the principles I studied, the policy that stood out the most was always the principle that "quality always beats quantity." One piece of content that converts at 10% to 20% is going to be much better than ten average pieces of content that convert at 2%. The message all the top copywriters delivered was a completely different one from what I had seen or been " sold" elsewhere online.

And I loved the fact that the focus is on delivering value. That felt more in line with my inner values.

So I started again. Through learning, determination, and more than a little obsession at times, I became skilled at copywriting, search engine optimization (SEO), and traffic building. Through this process, I also met lots of successful, kind, and enthusiastic people who genuinely love what they do.

I learned that being good at this job happens by focusing on and asking the right questions, and connecting with readers, it's not about learning how to use sales lingo!

What I discovered was that it IS possible to build multiple streams of high converting targeted traffic through your content, WITHOUT burning yourself out because you think you have to keep writing ridiculous quantities of material.

The saying "work smarter not harder" very much applies to content marketing!

Good content builds credibility.

I am going to show you how I make copywriting fun, satisfying, and profitable. Rather than feeling like some robotic writing machine - writing with purpose. I'll show you how to write with less hesitation, fewer instances of writer's block, so it's easier to write content that's immensely satisfying to write for your readers to read!

Write quality content, and you'll earn your readers respect and trust, and their desire for your stuff will grow naturally. And yes...though this process, your content will start to convert more readers to buyers without having to write anything that suggests obvious selling!

Writing can be immensely rewarding when you inject your style, do your own thing, and stay authentic, aspiring to help your readers as best you can. Stick to your style, rules you can imagine, and cultivate yourself.

So thanks again for reading, and happy copywriting!

Part One

What Is Copywriting

The dictionary says, *"Copywriting is the writing of content, especially for advertising and for publicity releases."*

To me, that's a reasonably clinical description for what is a very fluid and emotive process. It's also a misunderstood term and, in my opinion, often misrepresented.

One of the biggest myths about copywriting is that you need to be a super salesperson with the gift of gab to write good copy. The truth is, you don't need to be a slick salesperson or master spin doctor to do master the essential element of copywriting: to connect with, relate to, and motivate your readers.

I look at copywriting as a bit like having a hidden

superpower: the power to persuade and influence a reader's perception. Rather than trying to twist peoples' arms (metaphorically speaking) and exaggerate the facts, your job as a copywriter is to use your understanding of your customers' needs and concerns to write content that will help them get closer to achieving what they want.

Specifically, your job is to earn trust, to prove to your audience that you can help them achieve their desired outcome. You'll do this by creating trust, building confidence, and demonstrating value by providing helpful content. You'll also take your readers through a specific process to develop the desire and determination to make a decision and take action.

Copywriting is not about fancy words, or about writing Pulitzer Prize-winning stories, it's about forging a connection with your audience. Riveting copy or content isn't about you (sigh). It's about your readers, what they want, and helping them overcome obstacles to getting what they want.

Through your content, you can focus on topics that get your readers excited. Align yourself with their perspective.

Stand alongside them against the things they dislike, then walk them towards an action.

Let's imagine you have a friend named Matt, who's always dreamed of buying himself a specific model of classic Corvette. Let's say you finally discover the car he wants and say: *"Hey Matt, I've just found you a 1968 limited edition L88 Corvette in fire red, your color!."*

Matt is likely to be quite interested in what you just said, right? He might go to check out the car, but will he want to buy it? That all depends on what it is about the car that Matt feels is important to HIM. Matt may have specific criteria that you may or may not know are important to him.

Matt may only like one particular Corvette model, a unit produced in the factory with limited edition orange upholstery. So whether or not he likes the one you have just told him about will depend entirely on whether it has original orange upholstery - as you are probably about to discover.

Like the Corvette example above, most things that people

want also come with hidden requirements. The catch could be something to do with the product; it could be something to do with the price or even the delivery options. There can be many reasons why a reader might not immediately act on an offer, and these reasons could well be well disguised.

The point here is that knowing who you are talking to, what precisely it is about the "widget" they want, what they want to avoid, and what's important to them, is the **only** way to understand how to motivate someone to do what you (and they) want.

Build a foundation of good copywriting on these principles.

You can only formulate a plan for connecting with your readers based on something you know and understand. If you can relate to your readers' needs, focusing on what they truly want in your content makes writing a whole lot easier. By following a template - a sort of paint by numbers format - you can deliver critical information to your readers in a concise yet engaging way.

By the time you have finished reading this book, you'll understand the formula for creating each piece of content relating specifically to your product(s) and service(s). You will be able to create content that comprehensively covers all the essential factors you need to need to include for your specific audience.

With all of that said, how about we refine the definition of Copywriting to *"building excitement and interest in your audience and then giving them logical reasons what they can justify that excitement so they can move towards action."*

It doesn't matter what type of medium you are writing for, the same principles apply.

You will be able to write in a way that engages the reader, so you are talking "TO" them and not "AT" them... (like a lot of sales copy we see today).

The late Gary Halbert was the master of writing sales letters written like a story. They kept your focus glued to the text, but at the same time led you, cleverly, to take a specific action.

By the time you've read this book and practiced the principles here, your copywriting skill set will start to become something that is second nature.

It's important to remember that the best copywriters are always taking readers on a journey to a destination. On this journey, the reader obtains a clearer understanding of what it is they want, with increased motivation and confidence to decide to buy a product or service.

If you are writing with the genuine intent to deliver a high level of satisfaction to your audience, then you are using your copywriting superpowers for good. Rather than trying to sell directly, you are focusing on fulfilling their needs along the way to delivering your product or service.

Think of your content as a playground slide. A reader arrives at the top of the page, like a metaphorical slide. Once on that slide, they are riding it to the bottom through a series of content tiers. These tiers are what you put in place to build desire, trust, and, most importantly, the confidence to make contact, make a purchase, or sign up to do something.

By answering the right questions throughout this process, you are helping your audience get closer to achieving their desired outcome. Offer them quality information and demonstrate how to get closer to what they want. It's much easier to do this when you have done your homework and know what your audience (readers) are genuinely interested in, and then provide them with something they can do or use IMMEDIATELY to take the first step.

By taking the time to learn how you can help them and by demonstrating value before they buy anything, you are earning their respect and trust while helping to remove obstacles to their goal.

Give them something satisfying to demonstrate your intent to help and that you can deliver what you promise.

Now let's get your master copywriting training underway!

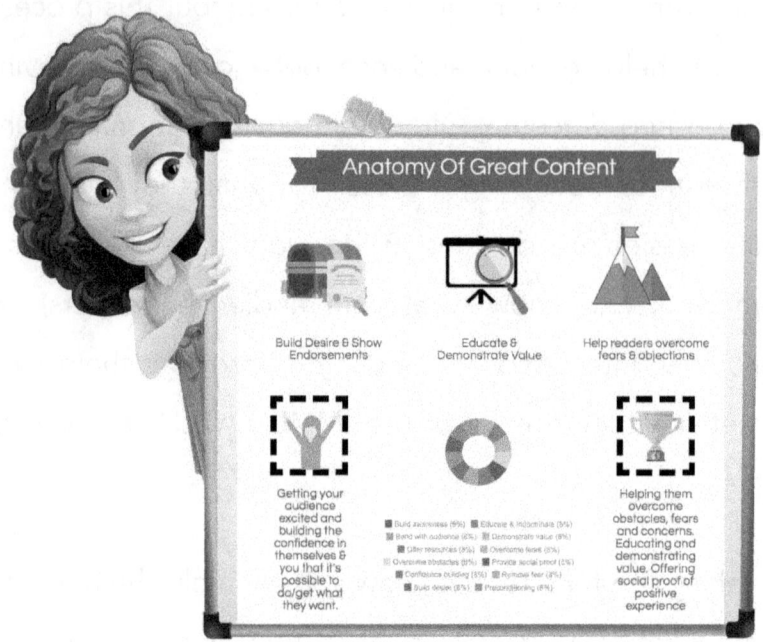

Elements Of Copywriting

Everyone who has a product or service to sell should understand all the various ways that their product or service can satisfy their customers/clients' wants and needs. They should know who it is they are trying to attract and what feelings, emotions, and emotional payoff they are trying to achieve as a result of buying your stuff.

If donuts were your favorite food and you were eating one now, how would you describe the taste and texture of that donut, and more importantly, how would you describe the positive responses you FEEL when you're eating it?

Similarly, how would you describe how your customers will feel when they buy your products or services?

- ◆ What problems do they solve?

- ◆ How do they solve them?

- ◆ How many different ways do they help them?

- ◆ What is unique and special about your products or services (or support)?

◆ How will buying your stuff improve their life?

You can dig deep into these questions. What positive emotions or results can the products or services you are promoting deliver?

The next question is: what uncertainties are currently preventing your potential buyers from investing in those products or services? What do your readers need to learn or understand - the features and benefits?

What assurances can you offer to gain trust throughout the buying process?

What do you need to do, say, or demonstrate to build desire and earn trust?

It's worth putting the energy into discovering all the different thoughts and questions a prospective buyer may have to help you develop a clearer idea of what you need to convey to your audience. Base your plan on solid research and a thorough understanding of their needs.

Once you have a clear picture, you can introduce who you are as a person, team, or company. Your audience is scrutinizing you (whether consciously or not), probably weighing up whether you are someone they want to pay attention to, someone they can trust, and respect. Understandably, they want to feel familiar with you first.

They'll gain this familiarity through your content. If you deliver value and your audience feels good by reading your content, it is more likely your readers will be willing to give attention to the next part of the conversation - and want to continue the metaphorical journey on which they about to embark.

Now's the time to begin placing the pieces of your sales letter & content jigsaw puzzle. In doing so, be yourself and give generously with facts, useful content, and answers to their most pressing questions.

AUDIENCE
Who are your audience
What do they like,
dislike & talk about
What is their
desired outcome

DESIRED ACTIONS
What action do
we want them
to take.

GOAL or AIM
What is the desired
outcome you want to
achieve. What action do
we want our audience to
take?

COPY

BENEFITS to AUDIENCES
Relate products &
services to the audiences
needs & desires.

STRATEGY
How to present
copy to your
audience

FEATURES & BENEFITS
What does the product
or service do?
How does it work?
What is special about
the product or service?

Traits Of Top Copywriters

For me, copywriting has always been about connection. Connection starts with establishing a comprehensive understanding of needs and what your audience MOST WANTS as the desired outcome.

It's equally about helping your readers make sound, informed decisions and helping them to avoid pain. Finally, it's about guiding them to a destination that can deliver them to what they want.

All copywriters need to develop an acute awareness of all the fears and concerns readers have behind their desires. Understanding how a reader wants to FEEL by buying what you are selling is key to connecting with them. Is it for monetary, time, ego, pride, or social reasons? Are they buying it because they want some emotional payoff? A buyer might be purchasing a new smartphone because they NEED it, but the real question is always WHY do they think they need it, and HOW does it improve their life?

We know they want something, but with every want comes a fear or concern. A new potential buyer doesn't know your company, and you haven't earned their trust or demonstrated value yet. The reader may also be scared of making the wrong decision, so you must help them address their fears as part of the process of deciding whether or not to make a purchase.

Copywriting begins with understanding what satisfaction 'looks like' to your specific audience, then continues with a mindfully crafted narrative to overcome obstacles and demonstrate your benefits to them.

Top 10 Traits Of Good Copywriters:

1. Customer-Centric

2. Aware Of They Own Biases

3. Language & Tribe Research

4. Value Centric

5. Not Scared Of Elephants

6. Imperfect

7. Clear And Concise

8. Consistent and Congruent

9. Qualification - Talking To The Right People

10. Checklists And USP's (Unique selling propositions)

Customer-Centric

If you study the intent and styles of successful copywriters, you will notice that they are highly customer-centric. That means their focus is on a customer's desires and all the different ways the customer wants to achieve those desires - but also avoid pain.

They also know how to deliver perceived value BEFORE they ask a reader to buy anything.

Aware Of They Own Biases

Copywriters should be aware of their own bias towards a product or service.

Just because you love something about a product or service, it doesn't mean that's the same reason your readers will. Top Copywriters talk to the reader's view of a product or service and filter out their own biases.

When writing about the benefits of a product or service, it is crucial to research what customers are saying. Learn the good, the bad, and the not-so-obvious points of the focus of your audience. Please don't assume that what you like is their reason for buying.

Language & Tribe Research

Audiences are a little bit like tribes, or clubs & sports teams.

Tribes hang out together, sharing activities and talking about the things for which they have a common interest. They often have lingo or specific terms to describe tools or other aspects of their interests. They usually have mutual likes and peeves too, and they will actively talk amongst themselves about both what they like and dislike.

Developing an understanding of the language and an understanding of tribes is vital to connecting with them.

Value Centric

Good copywriters believe in delivering something of value early to satisfy the desire for instant gratification and to establish immediate credibility. The little good deeds you do when someone reads your intro can demonstrate to your reader that you understand what they need and that you are most likely to be the best person/company to deliver this.

If you can offer small yet helpful chunks of information and resources BEFORE they buy anything from you, you are not just another marketer presenting another marketing pitch, but someone who is already proving what value you can deliver.

You are proving that you're serious about your intent to help, that you actually can help, and that you are a credible source of information.

Give your audience a taste of feeling good, so your readers will be much more likely to want more.

Not Scared Of Elephants

Why not address the big scary elephant in the room?!!! Good copywriters are happy to be the superhero. They dare to take care of the elephants for their readers. Their elephants being all the fears and concerns the readers have around a potential purchase. Don't be afraid to address these concerns rather than gloss over them or, worse still, completely ignore them.

Readers want someone to recognize their concerns and are not scared to deal with the things mere mortals (and not superheroes) are too scared to tackle on their behalf.

Imperfect

Nobody is perfect. People are much more likely to relate to and trust someone willing to say, "hey yep, I was a dork and screwed up." We respect someone happy to admit their mistakes openly.

We also like to avoid pain wherever possible. Let's face it; we don't like being the first to take a potentially dangerous leap if we can watch someone else do it first.

If someone's already made it safely and happily through something you were scared of, you are likely to want to learn how to avoid any mistakes they made along the way. If they then showed you a more comfortable, faster, or more satisfying way to achieve what you want, you'd be grateful.

Good copywriters are happy to make damaging admissions about past mistakes and share the valuable lessons they've learned. If a writer is honest enough to admit their mistakes - no matter how embarrassing they may be, readers may relate to the situation, perhaps chuckle, and hopefully want to utilize the lessons learned from it.

Clear And Concise

Copywriters are careful and precise. They value their audience's time and recognize that they may have just one opportunity to align with readers and begin to earn their respect.

Consistent and Congruent

Just as crucial as being transparent, being consistent also keeps a reader-focused. Building familiarity also builds trust. If you're talking about a specific thing in a particular way or asking a reader to take action, that message needs to be consistent across the whole of their content, so readers feel secure.

For example, asking someone to "sign up" on one part of the page and then "to register" on another, even if you are effectively asking them to do the same thing, can be enough of a change in wording to confuse them. Keep the same continuity of language and instructions.

Please don't make the reader work hard to understand what is required of them to take the next step.

Checklists And USP's (Unique Selling Propositions)

How many times have you walked into a store or looked for something online, liked what you've seen, and then left that store so you can do some comparison shopping for price or features?

Everyone wants to feel like they've gotten the best deal. It's human nature to want to feel like you've won.

Giving a reader not only a list of a product or services' features but also a list of unique benefits that only your company offers makes it harder for the competition to compete.

When done thoughtfully, this is a compelling way to position a brand, product, or service.

Qualification - Talking To The Right People

Good copywriters will tell you it's much better to qualify buyers first and talk specifically to them, rather than try to sell to people whom the product/service isn't the right fit for in the first place.

Once upon a time, I used to write long copy sales letters for digital products sold on the Clickbank Marketplace. They rank businesses partly on their refund rates, the lower, the better. So to keep our refund rate low, it was necessary to eliminate people who didn't meet OUR criteria. We ONLY wanted people to buy our products, which we knew we could help in a significant way.

We ONLY wanted the right people to buy, and we would come right out and say, "if you are looking for X, then this Y won't suit you." Being transparent about this was incredibly powerful from a credibility point of view, and it also ensured a much higher satisfaction rate from buyers.

We took an immense amount of care to ensure people understood what they were getting, why they should invest, why it was worth it from a financial point of view, and how to justify to themselves that they deserved it.

We also backed up the purchase with extra bonuses they did not expect to get so they were even more delighted with their purchase after it was delivered.

Good copywriters are not afraid to come right out and say, "Hey - is this you? If not - that's okay - you might find what you are looking for over here" (and send them elsewhere). It's not only honest - but it also solidifies your credibility to the people who ARE your buyers.

My Rules Of Engagement

I can't write sales and ad copy unless I believe what I'm writing. I need to feel like I'm genuinely helping someone learn or solve something through my content. I know that what I'm trying to sell may not suit everybody's needs, and that's okay. But if I have provided readers with some value, then no matter whether they buy or not, I feel I have helped them make the right decision. And if they become a customer, our relationship is already built on positive goodwill.

70% Psychology 30% Skill

Motivation Is Emotional

Behind every decision to buy, there is an emotional process that buyers go through mentally and emotionally.

People don't buy stuff based solely on logic; they buy because the things they want give them positive emotional satisfaction - an emotional payoff. In other words, the logical justification behind the sale happens after a combination of psychological, emotional, and rational processes.

Every step of the buying process must build on a reader's emotional reasons for buying, reinforced with logical reasons and justifications to buy.

Primarily two things motivate people: **the carrot or the stick** - the promise of gain or the fear of loss. The stick - fear - is always the more significant motivator (and needs to be handled carefully).

Think about this for a moment:

Which book title would you prefer if you suffered from acne?

"Acne Eliminating Natural Skin Masks"

Or

"Natural Soothing Skin Masks To Eliminate Embarrassing **Acne** & Get Clear Soft Beautiful Skin In 14 Days"

I could show you data to prove that the second title sells five times better than the first. Why?

Because it addresses several issues in one statement: it fulfils a need, negates a negative impact, infers a positive outcome, and specifies an expected time frame (14 days).

The emotional payoff in any title makes it much more personal and connects with what people want to FEEL as a result of buying the thing they want.

Remember that people want to:

◆ Feel popular or included by peers and society

- Feel abundant (or wealthy)

- Feel attractive

- Feel healthy

- Feel secure

- Achieve peace and happiness

- Have more time

- Have fun

Because they want to meet the human needs of:

- Certainty and Security

- Uncertainty or Variety

- Feeling Significant or Important

- Feeling Connected or Loved by Someone

- Growth and Contribution

- Contribution to the Whole (all of humanity)

- (We will be covering these in more detail soon).

These payoffs are what your readers want. What you are selling is just a channel for fulfilling their needs in some way. So your content needs to address your audiences' **specific human needs**. You need to link those needs to the benefits of your products and services.

Readers go through both conscious and subconscious processes to feel confident enough to make a buying decision. This process has not changed much over many decades and varying sales formats. The only real difference in this day and age is that the online shopper is less likely to read an ad, go to the store and eyeball a salesperson to help them decide what they want. They are more likely to buy online and have stuff shipped to their door.

Statistics show that customers are much more likely to shop online and maybe, but only perhaps, go check out a store locally so they can see, touch, and feel the item before they buy it.

If they can't SEE IT, FEEL IT, and TOUCH IT, then the logical, safety-conscious part of their brain, the part wired to test a situation for security and safety, will be more likely to challenge their emotional response. The "critic" in a buyer's mind will have a stronger influence over their buying decision than if they had walked into a store and used their other senses to make a decision.

In the (as my kids say) olden days before the Internet existed as a point of sale, you would walk into a store and speak to a salesperson. You would look for someone who looked like they could help you, someone who understands what you need. The first thing a salesperson would do would be to determine, quantify what you're looking for (and if you are a potential buyer, of course!.

At the same time, you would be qualifying the salesperson to establish whether they can give you the right information and whether the store carries what you want.

Let's imagine this scenario:

You are looking to buy a new television, and you visit the local electronics store to see what they have on offer.

Once you establish that you are in the right place, your next step is usually to find someone who has the expertise to discuss the features and benefits of the television that you are considering purchasing.

There is a qualification process for both you and the salesperson. The first thing you want to know as a customer when you walk into the store is whether or not that store can provide what you want. The salesperson will be establishing whether you are a browser or buyer.

Next, a whole bunch of other factors start to come in to play.

The salesperson has already greeted you with a smile and asked how they can help. At this point, you tell them your interested in TV's, and may even begin to mention some of the features you think you might like. If the salesperson is conscientious, before they take you to a TV, they will ask you a series of qualifying questions to establish which specific features and benefits you want and precisely WHY you want them. He/she will assess what it is that you want to experience from that television, e.g., movies, high-definition, Internet capability, excellent surround sound, etc.

You may or may not already know what features and options you want, and so the salesperson has the job of establishing these essential details. If the salesperson is good, they will try to help you associate these features and options with your desires. For example, a good salesperson, while talking about high definition, will take you to an HD TV playing the HD movies you have told them you like. A good salesperson will identify your "**turn on buttons**" - what it is that gets you excited. They will also try to ascertain your fears, concerns, and what you don't like about your current TV or any new ones you've already seen.

Next, the salesperson starts telling you what TVs he/she has on display in the showroom for you to survey. Hopefully, they will go on to explain all of the features and benefits of the televisions in question. You may, at this stage, start to get excited about a particular TV and start thinking: *"Hmmm, maybe yes, wow, that's amazing color and definition; this one will be amazing for watching movies."* This is the emotional part of this process. This is also usually when your inner sceptic starts to make an appearance. Enter the logical part of your brain. The next thing you start thinking is *"Hang on a second, how do I know this person is not just trying to sell me this particular TV so he/she can free up showroom floor for new stock, or that he/she isn't bluffing and pretending they are a TV expert"*.

You have reached the point where your inner skeptic ramps up the qualifying process with thoughts like *"How long has this salesperson been working here? Did the boss tell him/her to clear out this TV? What is this persons' motivation for wanting to sell me this TV? Should I trust their advice?"*. It's very natural to feel this way and correlates to our human need for survival and security. Skepticism is a healthy part of our brain's wiring.

So what do you do to qualify this salesperson further? Well, you may ask how long they've worked in the store, and you might ask him/her a few questions to determine what you need to know. You might ask them what they personally like watching. The point is you are looking for cues to establish his/her understanding of your needs and their credibility. You're looking for indicators to confirm that this is indeed someone who can help you and knows their stuff. You want to understand how the advice they are giving you relates specifically to you and your situation. It is a reasonable expectation for a salesperson if you're going to invest a large amount of money in a product or service.

Once you've established the salesperson's credibility, you move on to price and discussing what the store is willing to offer as part of the deal. At this point, you may ask yourself what price other stores might provide for the same TV. You may wonder, *"But can I get a better price elsewhere?"* which is, of course, a natural question to ask.

If the salesperson has done their job, they will have explained any benefits of their offer over the competition. It might be that they provide a new extended guarantee period, bonus items, or even better, a one on one lesson from the salesperson or technician on how to set up their TV with personalized settings.

Price should not be the only consideration. As we all know, getting the best deal doesn't necessarily mean the lowest price.

A good salesperson will want to emphasize any non-price-related benefits to a potential buyer. They'll give the buyer a shopping list to go away with, whether metaphorical or actual. Preferably, he/she wants the buyer to have a mental picture of their offer, so when the prospective buyer goes comparison shopping, your list of 'must-have extras' pops into their mind.

Offering something like services or training that's unique to that website/store/person makes it hard for a competitor to compete with an offer. The value that a buyer will receive (over and above the price) should be something that's difficult to match. Comparison lists are a potent psychological tool to use in your sales copy.

Now let us move on to the close. Your salesperson has gotten you excited, taken you through all of your questions, concerns, and objections, and you are motivated to buy.

Now he or she asks you how you want to go about making the TV your own. They ask if you wish to purchase it today so you can get started and [insert the thing that made you excited about the TV]. They ask if you would like to know about their interest-free terms or paying cash.

At this point, a good salesperson will remind you of all the reasons why you want the TV and also give you ideas to justify the purchase. The salesperson might mention that this deal is only available for another three days at this price. They might even say the bonuses are limited to a certain number, or available for a limited time and ask you when you would like to come in for your free setup session. You may make your decision to buy - or not - at this point.

The above example is a typical example of the process you might go through when purchasing a real brick and mortar store.

The same thinking and emotional processes occur online; they just happen in a different format; that format, of course, is online media.

Next time you prepare to write content, your online research can be likened to the TV salesperson asking questions about what the customer wants. Your homework is key to writing content that helps you qualify who your buyers are, as opposed to people who are just browsers.

Later in this book, you are going to use your research to create a model for your actual sales letters, blog post, or social media content. While creating templates, think about all of the things your reader may be going through, like in the previous fictional TV buying example.

Your research enables you to create content that deals with reader questions and helps them through any obstacles on their way to achieving their desired outcome.

Focus on the psychological process of your readers, and the content will flow.

In other words, imagine the process your reader is going through, and how they may be responding - both emotionally and logically to your statements.

Imagine you are reading their body language and their expressions, try to get a feel for what they might be wanting to know (having just read your last segment of text). You can also refer to your Q&A research, so you also have a detailed list of known questions you can relate to the point you are currently working on.

These are a few things to keep in mind as you work your way through your copy/content zig-saw puzzle. If you keep an open mind - stay curious about who you are talking to, and what they need, a lot of ideas will start to pop into your mind as you write.

PART TWO

Writing With Purpose

Before embarking on any content writing project, it's vital to know what you want to achieve.

Whether it be to educate, demonstrate benefits, or to build desire, your intended message should have a clear purpose.

You need to know what action you want your audience to take as a result of interacting with your content, then plan out what you need to give them to get them there.

If you know what you want your audience to do when they arrive at their final destination, you can reverse engineer what steps you need to take them through to achieve that outcome.

Define a clear purpose for your content, then create your content path.

Research: Homework Is Everything

We have already established that researching your audience is crucial to everything you do. Proper research helps you to come up with a list or a series of steps your readers need to go through to feel confident enough to take the action you are asking them to take.

By addressing everything they want to feel as a result of buying your products and services, and also taking them through a process that removes hesitation and obstacles, you are increasing their motivation to buy.

Creating content is a formulaic process with predictable steps based on everything you know about your audience.

The number of objections you need to cover will be determined by what you discover in your research about your specific audience. By writing down everything, all your target audience is talking about online, both positive and negative - you'll be able to craft paragraphs that address these points one by one (or in many cases combine them).

Speaking to your audience in a language they recognize,

and a style they can relate to, helps them to feel like they're talking to a member of **their tribe,** rather than some Joe Bloggs salesperson.

There are many motivating human factors you will read about in this book that you can use to determine what might drive people to do what they do, and buy the kinds of stuff you sell.

Why not start by looking at places where your audience's tribe hangs out. Popular sites where people voice their opinions on Amazon, eBay, forums, and communities, which I will get to in a moment.

Find out what your potential customers talk about online. What do they love, what do they hate, what goals are they trying to achieve by purchasing XYZ product or service? Write down all of the things they talk about most, then make a list of all of the things that are most important to your potential customers.

What do they love, what exactly is it about the **XYZ thingamabob** they like? What answers satisfy or impress them the most? Write it all down so you can refer to it later. These notes are what you are going to be working your content around. The more thorough you can be the better, because the more specific the information you have to refer to, the easier it will be to create relevant and engaging segments for your content.

By now, I'm sure you understand that researching your audience is crucial to everything you do. Proper research helps you to come up with a list or series of steps your readers need to go through to feel confident enough to take an action you are asking them to take.

By addressing everything they want to feel as a result of buying your products and services, and also taking them through a process that removes hesitation and obstacles, you are increasing their motivation to buy.

Creating content is a formulaic process with predictable steps - built on everything you know about your audience.

The number of objections you need to cover will be determined by what you discover in your research about your specific audience. By writing down everything, your target audience is talking about online - both positive and negative - you can craft paragraphs that address these points one by one.

What you need to give them is a preview of the end game: the emotional feeling, or the payoff that buying your stuff will give them.

Start by looking at places where your audiences' tribe hangs out. Common sites where people voice their opinions are on Amazon, eBay, forums, and online communities. The juiciest ones are often found simply by doing Google searches for your competitors' products using specific search operators (which I cover later).

Find out what customers are talking about online. What do they love? Who do they like, and why? What do they hate? What emotive goal are they trying to achieve by purchasing XYZ product or service?

Write down (or create a worksheet).. .all of the things most talked about, then make a list of points that stand out as most relevant to your potential customers. What do they love, what exactly is it specifically that they like? What do they get to **feel** by buying it?

What answers give them the most satisfaction? Taking down these notes is critical because these questions and answers are what you are going to be working your content around.

Qualification & Credibility

You wouldn't take a plate of steak to a vegetarian pot luck dinner, and equally, you wouldn't try to sell a gas heater to someone who lived in Fiji, right?

So then why do so many online businesses spend so much of their marketing budget trying to reach people who are not interested in buying what they have to offer?

The generally accepted idea for many marketers when promoting websites - especially on social media - is to broadcast lots of content to as many **potentially** interested people as possible in the hope that a percentage of them will become buyers at some point. A reach as many people as you can plan seems like a plausible strategy. Still, it's very costly to promote content unless not precisely targeted to your intended audience.

Although we often get sold on the concept of 'targeted' marketing, the definition of what targeting means is not clearly defined. Marketing Sherpa research shows that average conversion rates online are around a tiny 1% to 5%. If that's the case, it shows that only a small percentage of website visitors become buyers. The other reason is that people who are buyers are not finding enough of what they need onsite to become leads or customers.

Part of the reason for this is that conversion experts do not design most websites and so pages aren't structured to convert as well as they could. The more significant issue, however, is that people don't do enough research on their audience before creating their content. They also forget or are simply unaware of the importance of preconditioning an audience offsite before receiving them onsite.

Fact - did you know that up to 61% of website traffic is non-human?

It is through your research process that you can adequately compose a seamless transition for your readers from the interested audience to a happy customer. Start by using offsite content to satisfy the intent and then follow through with continuity of related helpful content onsite - effectively walking readers to a sale.

If you are targeting the wrong people in the beginning, then much of your marketing dollar gets spent trying to sell to people who were never interested in the first place.

You want people who are explicitly seeking the benefits of the products and services you are selling to come to your website. Attracting these people means putting your energy into finding and helping the people who can benefit the most. Serving your audience through your content, and ultimately through their purchase of your products and services.

A targeted audience wants what you have to sell, and they want someone to help them pick the best solution for their needs. Your job is to show them that you are the right person/company to make that purchase.

Think quality, not quantity. Don't get fixated on the number of visitors to your site; more only equals better if they are **qualified** visitors. Remember, it's your research that will help you to decide who are the types of people to target your content and landing pages for.

Browsers, Shoppers & Buyers

There are several different varieties of potential buyers online, and many various reasons people use the Internet to find what they want. Sometimes it's purely for social reasons, other times to research products and services to fulfill a want or desire or to solve a problem.

People buy stuff to feel something. It's not categorically the THING they want, but the feeling or outcome that the thing will give them by having it.

Some of the reasons they may give you include:

◆ brand association

◆ comfort

◆ style

◆ looks cool

◆ to be trendy

◆ like the color

- to solve a problem

- to make life easier in some way

If they are looking for a service online, they might be buying it to:

- have more time

- impress the boss

- work more efficiently

- feel more in control

- make more profit

- save money

The point is behind every search; there is a desire to FEEL some payoff from buying it. Start with why, where, how, what, when intent-based questions. These questions can help stimulate a whole heap of reasons why people might want your stuff.

Remember that behind every search for something is an

intent you need to familiarize yourself with to be able to **satisfy that intent with your content!**

There are generally three different types of audiences: browsers, shoppers, and buyers. These audiences all have different intents - or, more specifically, are all in different phases of the buying process.

Browsers are online with no immediate intent to buy; for example, they may be visiting their Facebook page or reading the news. This group of online users may see something they then become interested in buying while browsing, but they didn't begin their online session with the intent to purchase.

The next group is **the shoppers**. These are people who have already shown some interest in a brand or type of product or service. They may not yet have a specific idea of what they want. Instead, they have a general interest in the brand, type of product, or service. For example, they may like Nike shoes but are not sure what style and color they want. These people are just looking around to try and narrow down the best option. I call these people shoppers.

Next up are the hottest group of surfers who are what I call **buyers**.

These folks are the ones that know what type of "thing" or "service" or even brand they want and what specific features. They may have an idea of the benefits that product or service needs to provide to fit their requirements. These people are in a different frame of mind than browsers and shoppers.

They already have **the intent to buy** and are looking for indicators of **value and trustworthiness.** They are trying to ascertain who is most likely to give them the most favorable result. They aren't necessarily buying based on the best price, but possibly the best value. They're looking at which company can best deliver what they want. They are sensitive to your handling of their wants, fears, concerns, and desires. They are very discerning and will likely be scrutinizing you, both consciously and subliminally.

Generally, there are only two reasons "buyers" who

arrive on-site won't buy:

◆ they don't want what you have or

◆ they don't understand or believe that you can deliver what they want (or don't trust you can provide the best value at that time)

Why it's essential to define and categorize different online users.

Remember that people are usually using the Internet for one or more of these reasons:

◆ to solve a problem

◆ to find something they want

◆ to be entertained

◆ to connect with other members of their tribe in some way

Just like clubs, groups of friends, social groups, online users generally hang out in tribes. Every tribe has its personality, etiquette, language, shared interests, plus pet likes, and pet hates.

Your job as an online marketer is to determine which online groups are closely related to your product or service. Who are the most likely characters in those groups you can best satisfy? Then meet them WHERE THEY ARE AT in their buying process.

Ask yourself: - "Out of my target audience, who are the people to whom I can deliver the MOST value to though my content?".

Next, we will move on to questions you can ask to establish who these people are and what they want.

Who What Where Why When How

We have already established that before starting your content, you need to do your homework, so you know your audience's wants and concerns. You need to know where your audiences hang out, who they are, and how they talk to each other (the language they use). If you know what they want, how they want it, and, more importantly, how they are searching for it online - it is easier to create content that resonates with them.

You can demonstrate that you acknowledge them, understand them, and speak the same language. Help your readers get past their fears and concerns - help them find the right solution.

Find the people who want what you have, then DEMONSTRATE that you are the best source to deliver it.

Remember, if you don't feel you can deliver excellent value and genuinely help them, they are NOT your customers.

Research

Begin your research by asking the right questions. Asking the right questions helps you form a clear understanding of your audience and what they need from you to be comfortable making a purchase. It's much easier to create content when you are following a guideline keeping content aligned with your audience's needs and behaviors. It's also important to know whether you are talking to a browser, shopper or buyer, and remember, meet each group right where they are in the process.

The Who's, Wheres and Why's...

Who

Who is your audience? Who do they like associating with and why (who are their peers in their tribe)? Do they fall into age or income demographics? Who and what don't they like, and why? Write down a description of your audience and what you think is important to them based on what you have learned in your research. List these discoveries, write them down so you can refer to them close at hand.

What

What does your audience talk about, positive or negative? What are their passions? What is MOST and least important to them? What solutions are they looking for, or what desires are they trying to fulfill?

The process of writing this down will help you focus on the priority, the importance of different motivations your audience has for buying. What are the features they most like and dislike about competitors or the products you are representing? The most critical next step is to write what they want and what they want to feel FEEL.

What payoffs are they talking about getting from products and services?

Why

Why does your audience want products and services like those you sell? Why are they looking where they are looking to find what they want? What is the payoff? Ask why questions to refine further the emotional payoff they are seeking.

Where

Where do they hang out? Which websites, forums, communities, or clubs do they frequent? Where do they spend their time? Knowing this helps you refine and qualify the best places to put your content. If you know where your audience members hang out and what they like about visual formats e.g., images, or bulleted forum posts, then you can better tailor your content. If you know what your audience loves reading and where they like reading it, you will then understand what your content needs to contain.

When

When does your audience read content they like? Is there a time of day or night they are commenting in forums or online. **Please pay attention** to **when** they responded to something. If you see a pattern while doing your research, note it down so you can plan the best days and times to post.

How

How does your audience go about finding information? How do they ask for it, and what language do they use:

what words, phrases, and terminology? In which ways are they asking for what they want, because it helps you write in the proper context when answering their questions.

Now answer these questions in the form of solutions. What can you provide to give them satisfaction? What are they asking for, and how can you deliver that?

Keywords

Choosing keywords like "best XYZ widget" is one way people search for things, but did you know that **80% of searches** are in the form of a question such as: 'what's the best XYZ widget.'

From your audiences' point of view, they don't necessarily know what they require as a solution. All they know is that they want something or to solve a problem. It's necessary to take off your "seller goggles" and think from your audience's perspective.

Use the questions and language your audience members are asking. Use their language to craft copy that aligns with what they are asking and how they are asking it. Statistics show that long tail (longer than three words) phrases that also include a question or ask for a solution associated with a specific product or service are a lot more likely to be used by someone who is a buyer rather than a browser.

Use reviews and the types of solutions your audience members say they enjoyed to refine and format your keywords. There are many tools online you can use to learn how many people are searching for specific phrases. Remember to combine product or service-based terms with why, what, how, when, who type queries. My favorite is Keyword Atlas.

And remember the three types of online searchers: **browsers, shoppers**, and **buyers**. Wherever possible, you want to write content for shoppers and buyers. Use titles that shoppers and buyers are using and watch your reader retention click through, and conversion rates skyrocket!

Technical tips for using Google search operators to find content to research

Google is many copywriters' first port of call for researching to find their audience. Did you know you can perform custom searches to find specific topics using Google's advanced search operators?

Here are some searches you can perform using search operators to find reviews on products you are going to be writing about:

- ◆ Use "quotes" around "text you want to search" or use + word1 + word2 + word3

- ◆ Search a website for specific text use: site:example intext:"example text"

This one allows you to find a keyword on a specific website e.g. Amazon. An example you could add to the search bar would be

site:amazon.com intext: "blue nike trainers"

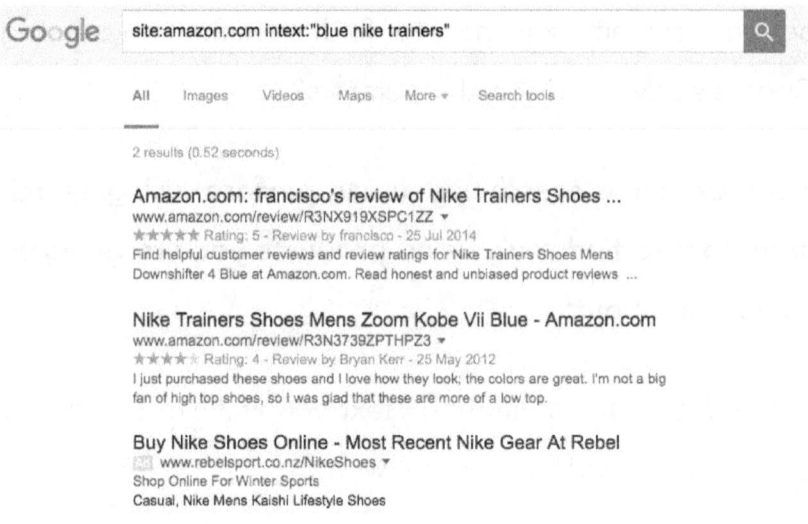

◆ Search for the keyword in any web pages, you can use:

intext:"canon + 6D + reviews"

Intext tells Google to search any page for the word combination of canon, 6D and reviews.

◆ Search for a keyword in a website URL specifically, you can use:

inurl:"add + your + text + here"

This is useful for when you want to look for review pages, for example, inurl: "canon + 6D + reviews."

- ◆ Search for a keyword in sites **excluding** your own (or another) use:

"keyword" -site:thesiteyouwanttoexclude.com

- ◆ Search for a specific type of file you can use:

site:example.com filetype:.pdf

- ◆ Search for a specific type of domain (universities for example which use .edu) use:

site:.edu "keyword"

- ◆ Another way to search for a specific type of website is:

inurl:forum+review intext:"canon+6d+camera".

This type of search tells Google you only want it to return results that have the word "forum" in the URL, and 'review'. I could leave out the review part if I were happy to look at comments in a forum, or I could swap out the word "forum" for "review" if I wanted to search for reviews only and not forums.

- ◆ Search titles of pages (the websites meta title description) you can use:

intitle:canon+6d.

- ◆ Search for specific text in pages on a specific website you can create your combination like:

site:amazon.com intext: "canon+6d+camera"

These operators help you quickly identify and sort from the millions of pages, the select few you want to read.

I use search operators all the time to find specific types of content and reviews. I even use them to find problems people are dealing with by using the operators:

inurl:forum intext:problem canon+6d or inurl:review

intext problem+canon+6d

(in this last example I want Google to search for canon and 6d and problems in the whole page, but the page URL needs to contain a review).

Notice that I used quotes around the text to get specific and include any combination of those words.

(Search for Google search operators in Google to find more options.)

If I also use a + between them, then keywords with any other words in between the text will be included in my results too. Look for reviews, forums, community, and anything else that is pertinent to your topic.

These operators are a researchers' best friend, and with a little practice, you can use them to find almost anything online.

Keyword Atlas is a tool I LOVE for keyword research in Google, Youtube, Amazon, and many other platforms. https:///keywordatlas

Social Proof

The definition of "social proof" is *"Visual or verbal proof that you can deliver the results someone wants, demonstrated and proven by customers and peers."*

Testimonials, reviews, customer feedback, case studies, and recommendations are all examples of social proof.

Social proof is another vital ingredient in your copywriting sandwich! Why? Because it's essential to show that other people have taken the plunge, that they have bought what you are selling, and have been very happy with the results.

What's even more important is to demonstrate **how** your readers can get the same satisfaction. Give them an example, an example of how previous buyers' experiences and positive outcomes may apply to them.

Social proof gives potential buyers a taste of what previous customers have enjoyed, while demonstration lets them FEEL it for themselves. This is a VERY powerful motivator for people. It's a bit like giving a kid an ice-cream. Giving them one nibble just makes them want to taste more.

You can also use images showing examples of people who are like your readers enjoying the benefits of your products or services. Photographs are a powerful visual tool to convey many messages all at once. They are a visual confirmation that it is possible to achieve what they desire.

Telling a story about how someone had an issue that your support team resolved quickly shows you are transparent and committed to customer service.

Use different forms of social proof on your page wherever possible. Don't feel like you are limited to one. Use images, customer reviews, case studies, and refer to customer situations as examples where appropriate.

Break it up to give your reader a "three-dimensional view of your credibility."

Authority & Positioning

Many successful online marketers will tell you that positioning yourself as a credible authority is the most critical thing you can do to increase your perceived value to the market place.

"The importance of authority, positioning, and personal branding for professionals, business owners, coaches, and consultants cannot be emphasized enough."

Let's be clear: being an expert is not the same as being an authority. Being an expert is something anyone can claim. Unless it's backed up by social proof and positive influence, it's just a statement.

Your reputation as an authority is something you earn by demonstrating your expertise to peers. You can create the platform for those peers to solidify your status as an authority in your marketplace. A definitive "expert advisory" presence spread across many platforms is a great way to build the impression of someone with knowledge and expertise.

Why not plan out your brand. Decide what you want to be

known for, then go about demonstrating to your associates and prospects your ability to deliver immense value.

- Rather than presenting a generic picture, why not have a story, your mission, and share it.

- Rather saying you're an expert, show them and prove it by being genuinely helpful and useful to them.

- Don't just tell everyone about your successes. Instead, demonstrate evidence of that and help your readers come to a confident conclusion that's the case.

- Don't just be just part of the conversation, create the conversation yourself.

- Don't just follow the crowd; earn your authority.

- Do condition your audience to believe in you by helping them in small yet significant ways, and do it consistently.

- ◆ Do seek out and find as many ways as you can to demonstrate to your audience that you are an authority on a topic.

- ◆ Do keep your message consistent. As is true of many famous catchphrases, make yourself known for something unique to your brand.

- ◆ Do be generous, help others, and not just your prospective customers but also your peers, so they will want to share your stories and your messages.

- ◆ Do offer lots of helpful resources that could end up being viral. Downloadable's, statistics and other data, how to's, infographics and step by step articles are good examples.

- ◆ Do keep your branding: logo, font, colors, and tag-lines consistent.

- ◆ Do be yourself. Don't be afraid to express the unique aspects of your personality.

Establishing yourself as an authority is about being memorable, helpful, and consistent across all content and copywriting mediums.

Preconditioning & Pre-ciprocation

The dictionary defines preconditioning as:

"A condition that must exist or be established before something can occur or be considered; a prerequisite. To condition train or accustom in advance".

I define preconditioning (for content writers) as the art of framing your prospects' expectations and desires **before** they arrive at the intended destination.

Give your readers a planned-out path to follow, to an action.

Preconditioning does several things:

1. Creates a path that builds familiarity and confidence in you and your products or services.

2. Takes the prospect through a qualification process that helps to reinforce readers' desires. A process that confirms they need what they want and walk them through (past) what they want to avoid.

3. Gives you an opportunity to demonstrate value early

on. Giving your prospects something useful early on shows your intent and demonstrates your ability to help them.

4. It shows you understand what your readers want - and that you can deliver it better than your competition.

Preconditioning builds the foundation for a great relationship with your audience, a bond that you can grow.

Preciprocation is giving before you get

Preciprocation is when you give something to your readers before you ask them to do something. The more you preciprocate and provide value to your audience, the more credibility you build with them, and the more goodwill they may feel towards you. It also teaches them that engaging with you is a pleasurable and comfortable process. A process they will be more likely to want to continue with and maybe reciprocate in some way over time.

Preciprocating is at the heart of how strong online (and real-world) relationships grow.

Bonding With Your Audience

When you meet someone for the first time at a party or social occasion, it would be weird to immediately launch into a half-hour monologue about your life story and everything you are awesome at a minute after you've met someone!

If you have ever sat down next to someone you've just met who, a minute after meeting you, tried to sell you something, you know how much of a turn off those types of people can be. The "Me Me Me" narcissistic approach isn't the best way to win friends and influence people in the real world, yet I see this approach regularly in both online and offline advertising.

If you are meeting someone for the first time, you start with chitchat or by asking a few non-intrusive questions first, right? You may discover what you have in common and maybe what their interests are, right? Good listeners are hard to find, and those who are are good listeners are generally much more accepted than people who talk AT you. People feel included and important when someone takes an interest in them. It makes them feel validated and understood, and we shouldn't forget this when writing content.

Like a real-life conversation when we are getting to know someone, it's ok to ask a few general introductory questions, right? When you've gotten to know someone better, you might learn about some of the things that are important to them, and even some of the things that they like or try to avoid. I'm sure you'd agree that someone who has just met you for the first time isn't going to want to tell you their innermost feelings and thoughts without establishing some kind of connection first.

First, you need to earn their trust by developing a relationship with them.

Meeting people online though your content is no different. Being a good listener and carefully aligning yourself with your readers' interests is the art of copywriting!

Now imagine you're standing in a queue wearing a pair of stylish Diesel pants (yup these babies might be your favorite brand because they feel so comfy and make your derriere look good). A woman standing behind you says, *"Excuse me, I hope you don't mind me asking, but I love your jeans....are they Diesels?....where did you get them? They look great on you - I would love to buy some"*.

This person is a stranger, but they have created an instant connection with you by talking about something you both have in common. They have given you a genuine compliment and, perhaps inadvertently, touched on the fact that comfort is important to you when buying jeans. This person may be a stranger, but he or she is someone with whom you share a mutual interest. Most likely, you'd be happy to tell them the name of the store where you bought your pants. You are both members of a "tribe" that enjoys wearing comfortable/Diesel pants. Your reasons for wanting them could be different, but you still connected with that person for a moment on a shared interest basis.

Now imagine having a deep and meaningful conversation with a very close friend. That friend asks you for your advice about a big life-changing decision they need to make. Your friend trusts that you know them well enough to give an informed answer. You have shared information before, and that worked out well, they trust you, so they feel confident in asking you again.

The above scenarios illustrate our natural tenancies as humans to want to connect or feel understood before we are willing to make a decision or a commitment to do something. Making a connection with someone can manifest in many ways. All you need is one commonality to start the ball rolling. Being familiar with someone's wants and needs makes it much easier to connect with and relate to them.

So what does this have to do with copywriting? Think of the first paragraph of your copy as your introduction and the opportunity to connect. It's much easier to break the ice if you have something in common to talk about, especially if it's amusing or something that ignites recollection of something that makes them feel good. Sometimes an alliance can happen by having a moan about something you know they are frustrated about.

Tribes also do this amongst each other online. For example; Golfers have their lingo or nicknames they use with their fellow golfers. Gym and fitness fanatics might use language that includes words like curls or bench press. The people that want to buy your products and services are also likely to have their specific dialect.

That's why it's important to speak to your audience in the same language they use to talk amongst themselves about their wants, needs, favorite things, or pet peeves.

When starting up a conversation with readers online, talk to your audience about the things they're excited about or opposed to, and align with them.

It's easy to assume that you know your audiences' fears and concerns already. You may well do, but before you start writing, that's why it's still vital to do comprehensive research to ascertain all the different ways (terminology and context) through which people are expressing their wants and their concerns.

Remember: people buy things because they want to FEEL a certain way. What is their desired outcome? Do they want to feel sexier? Do they want to save time? Do they want to save money? Do they want to keep up with the latest trends? You need to know the trends and patterns that drive the desire for what you are selling. Most importantly, HOW are they expressing this?

Pay attention to your audiences' language patterns, tone, and how they describe what they want because these patterns are the juicy tidbits you can use to relate to your audience in your content.

If you're just talking to your audience from a seller's perspective, using sellers' language, and talking about all of the features of your products and services, you will come across as a salesperson rather than a relatable and authoritative peer.

Talk about how your audience is going to feel, not just about your product from a technical or logical point of view. Give your audience payoffs that they can relate to from the very beginning of your content, so they want to read on and find out more. Show them you have been in their shoes and so understand what's important to them.

All content needs to be client-centric, focused on **them** and **their** desired outcome. The way to ensure your writing stays client-focused is to ensure that throughout the process, you remain in touch with how your audience thinks and feels.

PART THREE

Blah Blah What Did You Say?

People are so overwhelmed with data that they can easily become numb to the messages we are trying to convey within our text.

Readers arriving at a page usually skim over text on the page, looking for something relevant to hook their attention. They are looking for a point of reference to confirm they are in the right place to get what they want.

Your headline is the introduction - and sales intro that leads readers into the rest of your article.

Sub-headlines give readers further confirmation that they are likely to find what they want on the page. A bit like when you first walk into a store and isle headings indicate where to find different types of goods, sub-headlines are signposts pointing to something the reader wants. The job of each sub-header is to hold a reader's attention and entice them into reading further.

Paragraph sub-headers should summarize a story's sequence, so the reader can jump from sub-header to sub-header and get the basic gist of the story.

You earn a reader's attention through your titles, sub-headers, and bullets. So these should accurately summarize what you are offering to help them do, get, or learn by reading your content. When a reader has qualified your article as relevant and useful to them, only then you have earned the opportunity to deliver the rest of your content to your reader.

Detail Orientated Readers

Detail orientated people are the type of folks who will be expecting detail!

These people expect you to answer every little question and cover everything they feel you are obligated to explain before they will trust you. They are very particular and may read every word and punctuation point on your page.

You can refer to other off-page resources, or add links to other pages (providing they open in a new window) so that the reader feels like they have access to "the fine print" if they need to.

Detail orientated people like reassurance that they have been thorough. They may even go back over a page several times to check they haven't missed anything. They like checklists and "box ticking".

Detail folks are quite often perfectionists, so errors like poor punctuation, spelling mistakes, or misaligned content may annoy them.

It's worth going over your content periodically with this in mind, and correct any little issues you find.

Things you most want to get right for these folks are:

- Correct spelling and grammar

- A link to a FAQ's page or list of common questions

- An explanation about who you are and why you are credible

- A link to testimonials

- A link to fine print material (terms and conditions for example)

- Fine print

- Correct formatting, punctuation, and grammar

Skeptics

These people are often cynical and will often want to fact check everything you say.

These folks need to see more than just testimonials; they want proof - evidence that you can deliver.

Forcing everyone else (who is not a skeptic) to read all the fine print may risk losing readers' attention. If you are writing a website blog page or sales letter, you can satisfy skeptics by adding links to pop-up windows or even external sites (that open in new windows) with further explanations on those pages.

Often just a link to more testimonials or credible sources like Forbes magazine, for example, is enough to satisfy a skeptic. Just the fact you are showing links to the information that's important to them shows that you are transparent and willing to provide proof.

Remember skeptics want access to all the information, even if they don't actually use it. Having a FAQ and Testimonials or Case Studies link in your navigation on your home page also helps, as do endorsement logos of other companies somewhere on the page.

Skeptics need the following from your content:

- Social proof in every form you can think of

- Demonstrations and/or examples they can test out for themselves

- Names and photos, preferably business names if yours is a business-to-business website

- Third-party endorsements and demonstration of authority

- Stats and figures from reputable sources

- Anything and everything you can provide for a skeptic, so they can check items off their mental checklist

Skippers: Skim Readers

Skippers are the ultimate skim reader. They are readers who want to get to the relevant points as fast as possible. They may decide to read more detail IF you have given them ample reason to do so. They will use your titles, headlines, pictures and bullets to get the feel of what the page is about, then head straight for the offer. They don't feel they need to read all the "fluff."

These readers are generally impatient: thinking they know what they want, and they want to go directly to it!

If you're writing a sales letter with an option to purchase something immediately, then you need to cater to skippers by making sure you add a reference to the essential features in a prominent place. Ensure skippers understand what is included or excluded in your offer, even if they haven't taken the time to read literally between the lines.

Place a concise summary of what they get close to the main offer. A feature summary is also helpful for non-skippers because you are demonstrating transparency and a preview of what a buyer can expect.

How to satisfy skimmers:

- Create stepping stones in the form of headlines, sub-headlines, and bullets for skimmers to "jump" to. Tell a story through the process.

- Make your text clear, use white space effectively to emphasize important points.

- Make the offer clear and the P.S. explaining what they get equally as clearly.

- Use bullet points to show benefits further.

- Use images to make points.

Get To The Point Readers (GTTP)

Some readers have particularly short attention spans. I call them Get To The Point Readers (GTTP).

These readers can easily be turned off by long copy. They want to get to the stuff they want as soon as possible, so it's essential to give them concise points they can instantly jump to, from one point to the next.

These readers are the ultimate definition of skim readers or "super-skippers," so you'd better give them an easy way to find what they want - FAST! Think of a person in a hurry - how would you get to the point if you only had a minute to say what you needed to say.

Sub-headers are crucial for holding impatient readers on the page, as are concise paragraphs.

Things your content needs to keep GTTP readers happy:

- Punchy, short snippets of information.

- Very clear titles & subtitles.

- Pictures and bullets to break up paragraphs.

- A clear call to action and reason for it at the bottom of the page.

- Tell your basic story through headers and bullets.

Mixing It Up

You may be wondering how to cater to all the different types of readers with one piece of content. The secret is to write your content, then scan it afterward, trimming it down as you consider the different types of readers who will be reading it.

Writing something that appeals to various readers may sound like a difficult task. Still, it's much easier to refine your content down to a concise, punchy arrangement of literary genius when you know who you are talking to and what they need.

It's better to include everything first, and then cut your text down to just what you need, without missing out on all critical factors you need to add.

PART FOUR

Why People Want Stuff

Humans are creatures of habit. We are programmed to survive and thrive by following patterns of conditioning to help us function in every-day life. We are wired for survival and also for identity; we have egos and a need to feel a sense of both self and belonging.

The programming and routines we follow daily make it easier for us to meet our needs but also to deal with the unexpected, and survive in this world.

Some of our programmings are necessary for daily survival without having to overthink. Imagine if every time you wanted to switch a light on, you had to learn how to do it every time. Imagine you had to rediscover where you stored your food every morning; life would be pretty stressful. Human brains are neurologically programmed to remember specific tasks by rote so we can focus on other, more important things and deal with the challenges we face in our lives.

In the stone age, female brains were wired with the capacity to multitask so they could prepare food and make clothes, etc. while keeping an eye on the children, so a saber-toothed tiger didn't eat one of them.

Male DNA was programmed to focus intently on focused tasks, such as hunting, so they could be effective in bringing essential food back to the tribe.

My point is: our DNA has us programmed for survival! This programming keeps us feeling safe or brings us closer to what we believe will improve our lives.

In the days of cave dwellers, important tasks included hunting and foraging for food. In today's age, the definition of survival is a lot more complicated.

When buying something, our "auto-programming survival supercomputer" is always whirring away quietly in our subconscious mind. It has a massive influence over our buying decisions and what our brains perceive as a danger in this modern age. We may not be worried about saber-toothed tigers, but instead, concern ourselves with other types of "predators." We think they may be trying to take our money (which to our cavemen DNA represents our ability to eat). They might be robbing our time without giving us something valuable in return. Our built-in survival mechanisms may present in different forms, but are very much alive and well.

People want products or services for lots of different reasons. These reasons may represent the need for survival or the desire to enjoy pleasure. You can refine these reasons down by paying close attention to the psychology of the audience for which you are trying to appeal. When you understand the psychology behind their desires, you can tap into their deeper motivations for buying.

We want to:

◆ Feel popular and included

◆ Feel abundant (or wealthy)

- Feel attractive

- Feel healthy

- Feel secure

- Feel peaceful and happy

- Have more time

- Have fun

Behind the desire to feel these things lies a set of human needs.

There are six basic human needs that we try, and sometimes struggle, to keep in balance. Most of these needs are unconsciously working away in the background and manifest themselves through our programming. Our programming is simply a mechanism to meet these needs, and our "survival program" controls every decision we make in life, including what we choose to buy.

So what are these human needs, and how they affect our actions when buying something? If you think about the feeling we want to experience, they all come down to one of these six fundamental human needs:

The 6 Fundamental Human Needs:

1. Certainty and Security

2. Uncertainty or Variety

3. Feeling Significant or Important

4. Feeling Connected or Loved by Someone

5. Growth and Contribution

6. Contribution to the Whole (all of humanity)

1. Security. The first need to feel secure and safe is a compelling one. It is all about security and safety. The caveman genes in all of us give us the instinct to watch for predators. The modern-day predator could be someone trying to fleece us out of our hard-earned money.

In our copywriting, we need to address this need. We need to prove to our readers that we have good intentions and that we are proficient at helping them get what they want.

2. Certainty. The second need is around wanting certainty, the need to know we can expect an outcome (more or less). Then there is the exact opposite of this coin, which is the need to enjoy something different and exciting. In copywriting, we can meet both of these needs. For example, to satisfy the need for a defined outcome, you can add case studies of other customers, or demonstrate this by systematically showing how your XYZ widget can produce the result the reader expects. Then to also satisfy the need for variety or something new and innovative, you can write about new developments and innovations, or something visionary (maybe it's something they recognize, done in a specific cool new way).

3. Significance. Feeling significant is another powerful driver. People want to feel they are valued and respected. So when you are writing content, think about how you can validate your reader. I'm not talking about being patronizing or schmoozing people. I am, however, saying that you can find a way to help your reader feel good about their decision-making process by adding in affirmation from credible sources that they are on the right track. An example of this could be adding a third-party endorsement that suggests, for instance, that people/a system is more intelligent, smarter, more efficient, or happier for choosing "insert a specific type or feature of a product or service" and **why**. If other people have been praised or validated for owning or using something, people naturally want inclusion in that group of "cool" or "smart" people. People seen in a positive way for donating to good causes is also an example of validation, not only from feeling good about making a contribution point of view but also because they are more likely to receive praise and gratitude from others.

4. Connection. Feeling connected and accepted is another essential need for people. It's a commonly accepted fact that having a sense of belonging is important for human growth and development. Being recognized amongst your peers makes one feel safe and happy. People will do all kinds of things to feel included. Clubs, hobby groups, and gangs are examples of peer groups that offer their participants a sense of belonging. This principle also applies to trends in fashion, sports, career paths, and even celebrity following by fans.

Create an opportunity through content for readers to connect with their tribe and, ideally, your products or services.

5. Growth. People want to grow and contribute to something bigger than themselves. We have all heard stories of people who have come from humble beginnings and achieved great things. Many of us have an underlying wish to do this, if only we could muster the courage or confidence required to do so.

Allow your readers to do something that will enable them to grow and extend themselves, to feel positive and hopeful about themselves and you too.

6. Contribution and philanthropy. This need generally applies to people who aren't living in survival mode. Many successful entrepreneurs who feel they live an abundant life want to contribute to a more significant cause than just their comfort. Like a donation box at your local supermarket, you can allow your readers to do something good for someone else. No wonder charity causes are so moving for people. You may not have the opportunity to do this directly, but you can try to think of ways to create useful content others want to share with their peers.

The human desire to be a better person, to help others feel a sense of belonging and inclusion is another example of contribution. We all want to be "seen" and to have the feeling we are "good." When given a chance - many will take the opportunity to do something good for fellow community members.

These are some positive, motivating factors to ponder. If you can touch on one or more of your readers' basic needs through your content, you will build a strong foundation to expand on. You can also appeal to ego-based emotions which we will cover in the next section "7 deadly sins".

7 Deadly Sins

Most of the time - as embarrassing as it can be to admit - we humans are very often motivated by ego. People want stuff or services for lots of different reasons, but you can guarantee that at least some of their reasoning will come down to some form of ego.

Writing sales copy, as we know, is a creative but also engineered process. It can be tricky sometimes trying to come up with ideas to correlate your content to a reader's needs and desires.

When looking for ways to resonate with an audiences' desires and concerns, you can refer to the six human needs, and you can also borrow from some of the oldest motivators in the book!

I'm referring to the Seven Deadly Sins mentioned in the Bible: They are pride, envy, gluttony, lust, anger, greed, and sloth.

- Pride is an excessive sense of ego and inflated belief in one's abilities. Pride is also known as vanity.

- Envy is the desire to have others' traits, status, skills, or situation.

- Gluttony is an inordinate desire to consume excessively to the point of more than what is required.

- Lust is an extreme craving for bodily pleasures.

- Anger or wrath is an intense dislike for or hatred of something or someone.

- Greed is the desire for material wealth or gains at the expense of the spiritual.

- Sloth is the avoidance of effort, of work - otherwise known as laziness.

Over the centuries, these "sins" have had their fair and justifiable share of bad publicity. There is a general assumption that anyone exhibiting one or more of these traits is devoid of morality, but this is not necessarily true. If we are honest with ourselves for one moment, every human operates with an element of these "sins." It's in our survival DNA, so we wouldn't be human if we didn't.

You can refer to the seven deadly sins and come up with some motivating triggers to highlight a benefit.

Use the seven deadly sins to come up with a whole bunch of ideas.

- How could your product or service make your reader the envy of their peers?

- How could your product or service make someone appear impressive to their peers?

- How can you appeal to their greed?

- How can you appeal to their laziness (sloth)?

You get the idea. So go for it - let your thoughts flow and have fun!

Giving Your Reader A Reason To Act

Little things can indeed make a huge difference in copywriting, and giving someone a reason or justification to take action is one of them.

Research done by Robert Cialdini from Arizona State University showed that giving people a reason why when asking them to do something increases their likelihood of doing it by multiples in many cases.

Researchers examined the donation process of the American Cancer Society, and how the last-minute change to the way they asked for donations delivered drastically different results.

The results demonstrate the need to analyze why people say "no," rather than just why they say "yes."

Donation collectors went door to door with two slightly different versions of donation requests:

The first request went as follows: "Would you be willing to help by donating?"

The second request went as follows: "Would you be willing to help by donating? Every penny will help."

Would you agree with the difference in how the question got asked seems minimal?

Although the wording may seem subtle, the variation in results was stunning.

Results showed that those who got asked the second variation were almost twice as likely to donate: 28% vs. 50% was the actual comparative ratio.

Cialdini's researchers concluded that people are much more likely to take action when given minimal parameters to follow.

This example highlights two things about the people donating. First, it shows that giving people a number to work with, in this case, pennies, incentivizes them to donate. Second, it shows that people given a reason, are more likely to justify doing something for a good cause.

An interesting thing to note is that the two groups donated the same amount of money! Yes, that's right, the second group of people was just as happy to contribute at the same level as the first.

And there is an even more fascinating story to add here. This theory has been tested across many profit-based business models, but also in situations where no money but rather when someone requested assistance. Another experiment involved a queue jumper asking to skip ahead of a bunch of people in a line. When they gave a reason, almost any excuse and used the word "because," a high percentage of people said ok.

You can use this concept in your copy. By adding words like "because" and combining these with phrases like "it will help you to _____", you can improve the conversion rates of your calls to action.

Part Five

The Important Stuff

As we have already considered, the essence of copywriting for any content is about your audiences' needs, wants, and concerns. It's crucial to do your homework BEFORE you pick up your pen or sit down at your keyboard.

I cannot stress this enough - it's your homework that will give you the ability to write fantastic copy, to write content that gives your audience the satisfaction they are seeking.

"A successful ad begins by entering the conversation already taking place in your prospect's mind," Robert Collier.

Good content also meets readers where they are at in

their internal buying process. Long copy sales letters stand out from other material and are generally more "in your face" than blogs, articles, or social media posts. It doesn't matter what kind of copy you are writing; you need to make sure you aren't pushing your readers past the point at which they are ready to be at.

After a while you'll write without thinking too much about it. It will become like muscle memory.

I also learn't to fly helicopters. Learning to fly a helicopter has parallels to learning to become a marketer and copywriter. A lot of the feel for keeping a helicopter hovering steadily, and flying in balance, smoothly, comes with practice and bedding in the skills over time.

Trying to mentally focus all the things you need to do

when you first learn to fly a helicopter is overwhelming. But over time, all of the fine tuning and micro-movements needed to fly, gets embedded.

Writing copy is similar. Practice these principles and writing compelling content becomes second nature.

Anatomy of good sales letters and sales content:

◆ Grab their attention with a hook.

◆ Build their interest.

◆ Offer something to explain who you are and why you are credible.

◆ Give them a features list which is also a "shopping list," so even if they decide to leave your page at that moment, they will be more likely to come back to you (because you've given them a list of things that make your offer more desirable than the competitions!).

◆ Back up everything with social proof. Include evidence to prove you are serious and can help.

- Remind your reader what they are going to get and add bonuses or limited extras.

- If you are writing a blog or other non-commercial or social media, summarize instead of explaining an offer.

- Use inferences (more on this later) and use endorsements or references to authoritative third parties.

- Add a P.S. and even a P.P.S. – I say this because it's still what many of the top sales writers in the world do consistently - sometimes they also include a P.P.P.S.

Most people I talk to who are new to writing copy, are relieved they don't have to be a cheap salesperson or write hype in any shape or form. It doesn't matter how smart or pretty a page is if your content doesn't connect with the reader - it isn't going to perform.

Content that gently addresses the reader's deepest concerns and demonstrates value is much more potent than any over-hyped copy.

Audience Intent

When creating Adwords and Facebook ads for clients, I always notice the highest converting ads are those that contain wording that closely aligns with a reader's intent, and then asks the prospect to take action that leads to satisfying that intent. When teaching people how to improve content ads, we always emphasize the importance of understanding readers intent before creating their ads.

When writing a blog or article content, it's no different. Keep your readers' intent in mind. Begin your content by entering the conversation that's already in the reader's mind.

Whatever questions or information your readers are seeking, you need to get precise about answering them. Rather than trying to please a broad spectrum of readers, in my opinion (and research shows) it's better to focus on a smaller sub-group, one with an identified, narrowly focused intent. For example, let's say you are writing about how to choose golf clubs; rather than writing one general article for everyone, it's better to pick out subgroups, and write several specifically targeted articles to satisfy the intent of each subset. You may write separate posts /articles on choosing golf clubs for women, tall people, or maybe different perspectives for different swing types.

By going straight to, and answering a specific problem in the mind of the prospect, you are giving the reader an instant payoff that they didn't have to search for through a whole page of generic material to find.

This way, you have a much higher chance of connecting with your reader, providing the satisfaction they want, and encouraging them to take the next step.

"You can't please everyone, nor should you seek to, because then you won't please anyone, least of all yourself." Dylan Moran

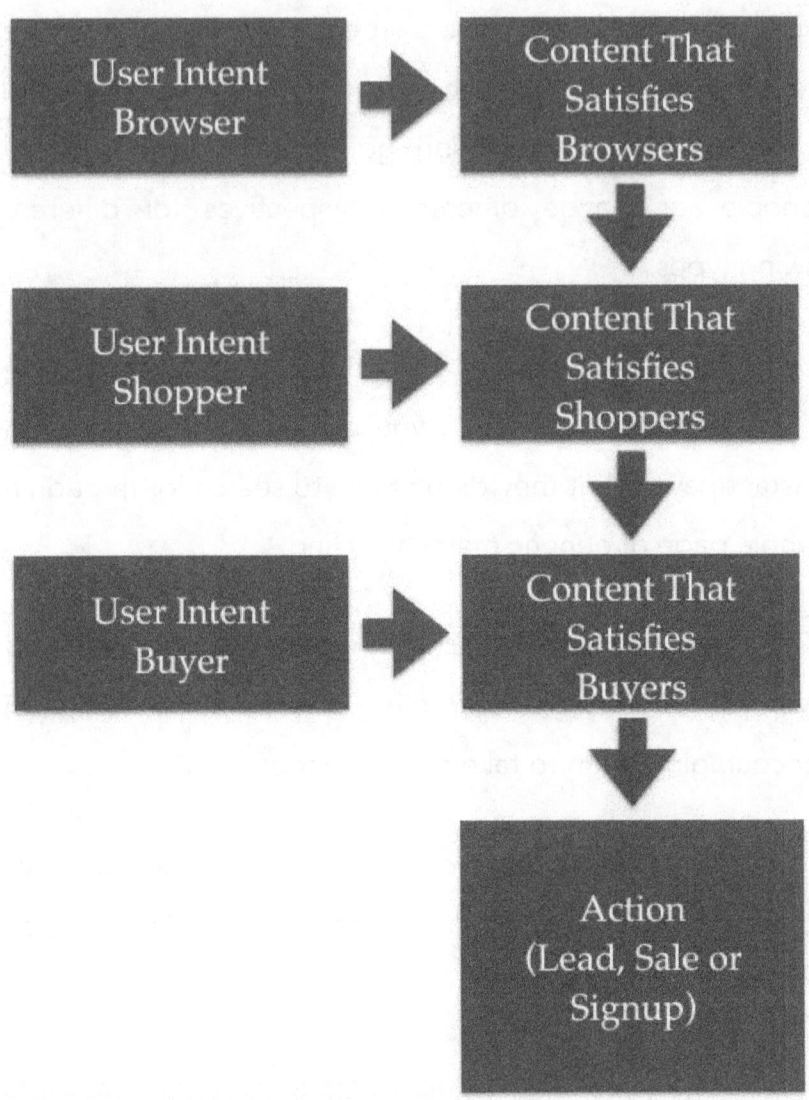

Overcoming Objections & Concerns

Many writers are understandably nervous about bringing too much attention to readers' fears and anxieties. They believe it will turn people off. Putting a reader off is only a risk if you don't quickly move them toward a solution for those fears and concerns. Studies show sales letters that address readers' concerns in an empathetic way are determined to be more trustworthy and more of an authority than those who try to gloss over potential issues.

Identifying and addressing objections creates an opportunity to deal with any hesitation the reader may have. Quite often, readers are not even aware of all of their concerns themselves, so if you haven't addressed issues not identified (but still there), it limits your opportunity to help your reader overcome them.

Talking about readers' fears does several things:

- Helps them identify any hidden issues they may have at the forefront of their mind (bringing them from subconscious to conscious thought).

- Shows the reader that you understand their

concerns, which validates them.

◆ Gives you an opportunity to walk the reader through and past the problem.

◆ It allows you to point out any positive points of difference between your company and its competition.

You can introduce objections in different ways. One way is to talk about solutions to concerns other readers have previously had in the form of a FAQ section. Another is to include a list of potential issues they may be facing and then tackle the solutions one by one.

You can talk about solutions to these common issues, but before you do, make sure you validate the reader by affirming that these are reasonable questions to ask.

The reason for this is that some readers may feel embarrassed, thinking that they might be asking silly questions, or if they are skeptical, it's a way to let them know you take their needs seriously.

It's human nature to want confirmation and reassurance

that you are taking the right steps (and asking the right questions). So go ahead and give your readers a heads up with something like *"Hey, you may be wondering* _____. *It's a question we get asked a lot because people want to get {insert safe outcome] but are afraid of [insert scary potential outcome]. We've done* _____ *and* _____ *to ensure you get [add positive outcome]"* without *"[negative experience]"* .

This statement not only validates their reasons for asking the question but also answers it in the form of an explanation that makes sense to the logical part of their brain. The statement *"does that make sense"* or *"makes sense right?"* can be used as a way to condition their subconscious mind. Asking whether your solution made sense, and therefore confirming you understand their initial concern assures them it's not something they need to worry about when buying from you/your company.

Talk to your audience as if they are sitting down next to you, asking questions. What if this happens or what guarantees you offer etc. Give them answers that are logical but also align with their emotional needs. Assure them that like them, lots of people had the same questions, and everything turned out ok.

Help your readers feel good about asking the question and about the positive outcome they can experience as a result.

The Importance Of Headlines

Headlines are the equivalent of a billboard advertisement for the rest of your content. Your headline needs to grab a readers' attention and include a hook that connects your content to their desire.

As discussed, the job of a headline is not to sell the product or service first up. Instead, it's purpose is to create the opportunity to precondition your prospect and lead them through the rest of your content. Remember, you want them to read your content like a slippery slide to the bottom of the page. Your content is leading them to the action you want them to take.

The headline is the metaphorical top of the slide.

Your headline should offer something and then (preferably) addressing their biggest fear or concern at the same time. For example:

"How to get this without having to do that!" (That being the thing they want to avoid in the process).

A headline needs to be clear and concise, punchy, and

descriptive and with definite intent. There are five basic types of headlines, each with a different purpose.

1. Urgent – gives the reader a reason to act now

2. Unique – saying something in a new or unique way

3. Ultra-specific – teasers to draw the reader in to a specific task set (Best time to _____, 4 foods that can _____, Ten steps to a _____, 5 things to avoid when _____.

4. Useful – this type of title appeals to the reader's needs

5. Controversial - appeals to audiences where there is a lot of discussion and controversy

Within the five categories, there are ten subtypes of headlines

Benefit: Benefits sell, features don't. Again: if you have researched your market well, you will know what benefits your audience wants to experience.

Command: Giving your audience a directive about what to do. You can also encourage action by offering a benefit to go with it.

Direct: Tell your prospect exactly what to expect and what you are going to do for them.

Guarantee: State a hot benefit and guarantee it. Of course, you need to make sure it is a decent guarantee and one that you can stand by.

How to: More than 7,000 book titles begin with 'How To' because they sell! When testing headlines, try adding a "how to" in them.

Indirect: Use curiosity to raise a question in the reader's mind. Use curiosity with caution, and give the reader a decent payoff to satisfy their curiosity, so they are delighted with their "discovery."

News: If your product or service is topical or newsworthy, use it in your headline.

Question: Introduce an industry or market-specific question. Again you have to be careful when using this one to position yourself as an authority and back it up if possible with 3rd party references. The best types of questions to ask are questions that engage your prospect in some way with something specific to them.

Reason Why: Give your prospect solid reasons why they should read your content.

Testimonial: Use excerpts from testimonials to write winning headlines with a benefit included. These are great for showcasing people like themselves who benefited or have been able to achieve something your readers want.

Remember: headlines are the sales pitch for the rest of the page. You don't have to sell the thing you are promoting through the headline; you only have to use it to entice the reader into reading the rest of your content.

The Art Of Inference

The best copywriters in the world use inference as a form of influence. Yup - they mess with your head by inferring something rather than saying it directly.

Let's say I am selling a type of office chair to an office manager and say something like:

"We find that the majority of office workers that used to suffer from lower lumbar problems and now use this type of chair say it's the best chair for maintaining good posture, and they like the fact it eliminates the risk of long term lumbar damage."

If I had said, *"This office chair helps with lower lumbar support and lots of our clients like it,"* it would not have the same punch.

The first statement inferred that:

Lots of people buy these chairs

This chair is a superior model to others

The staff no longer have sore backs, thanks to the chair

There is a group endorsement of the product (more powerful than one person)

If the reader has a sore back, they will relate to these people (who are like them)

This chair has incredible lower lumbar support

Using the wrong chair might cause some kind of long term damage

Now if I had tried to get "all salesy" and say something like:

"The lumbar3000 is our best selling, most comfortable chair" without telling them why, or inferring a reason, the person listening might think, *"Oh boy, here I go again with just another salesperson."*

By using inference in copywriting, you have the opportunity to say a lot without sounding like just another salesperson. You can interrupt a reader's pattern of thought with what I call a "pattern interrupt." A pattern interrupt is when you say something completely unexpected compared to what people are used to hearing. Interrupt disrupts skepticism and the usual pattern of the automatic shutdown that occurs when someone thinks you are coming at them with a pitch they are familiar with (the way they are used to being sold to).

Include statements that interrupt people at a point where skepticism usually enters the picture. Say something they are not expecting - for example, if they are waiting for you to say something about being the best in your industry, I could say, *"Hey, not everyone likes our product!"* What - why would I say that? *"We don't want our customers buying the wrong model because of [insert reason]* (maybe something that the competition does). *That is why you'll see a lot of discussion* (bad reviews on competitors' sites) *by people who have been sold an XYZ product without proper fitting. That's why we insist on taking the care to make sure we [insert selection process] and don't want people to buy until we know their XYZ will be perfect for them & have a 14 day trial period* (inferring that we make sure they are happy no matter what) *"*

It's much better to talk about how a product or service

may help them by using inference.

You can begin with something that is a story, an example of a situation, or talk about how XYZ helped _____ to _____ and what we learned from that is _____ (as a third-party case study).

Direct the readers' focus away from anticipating the sales pitch and draw their attention to being curious about what happens in the story or example.

Frank Kern is one of the highest-paid copywriters in the world. He is a master at the art of inference. Watch his videos. Despite his casual persona (he is a genuinely decent guy), nothing you see included in his videos is accidental. He crafts every word to put the viewer at ease, to build confidence and desire. He throws in all sorts of little comments, one of his favorites being "no shenanigans". He knows that a lot of things are going through a viewer's mind and that he needs to ensure he has dealt with everything he needs to cover before the audience feels comfortable enough to proceed. Top copywriters know that dropping subtle but important statements into content as Frank does with his videos is extremely powerful.

Don't be afraid to make fun of yourself - throw in comments that put your audience at ease. Let's say you know that many of your readers are scared of giving something a go because they lack self-confidence.

You could throw in a comment about how you used to be such a novice when it comes to _____, that you were the worst [insert what they want to be good at] in your class. You are aligning yourself with them and providing reassurance that you might be an expert now, but once upon a time, you too were a beginner.

"Hey anyone can learn this - man if I could become successful at _____, and learn how to overcome obstacles (and without having to try the pain in the butt things I tried) anyone can. Seriously, we don't want to take on clients who we don't know we can help get an amazing return from their investment".

Think about how you can convert negatives into positives by pointing out the lessons learned from a negative experience or by explaining how the negative experiences apply to specific situations (and not necessarily to the reader's case).

There are many many ideas you can dream up to drop into your content. Remember that the purpose of inference is to put your readers at ease, to relate to them, and help them feel confident in their ability to achieve what they want through your stuff or services.

Words that infer authority, success and effectiveness:

Proven

Tested

Researched

Statistically

Devised

Administered

Applied

Winning

Outcome

Affirmed

Confirmed

Cited

Stated

Outlined

Cautious

Careful

Qualified

Certified

Graduated

Confirmed

Suggested

Damaging Admissions

Savvy marketers understand the influence of a "damaging admission." The damaging admission is where the seller points out the flaws of the product or service they are offering. The truth is that no products, services, or offers are perfect and so it's natural for prospects to wonder, *"What's the potential downfall or catch?"*

Here's where you can use the power of admitting weakness to show your strengths.

In the mid-eighties, Cleveland State University researchers made an astonishing discovery:

The research team created two fictitious job candidates, Dave and John. For each candidate, they created identical resumes and two very similar letters of reference. The ONLY difference between the two: John's letter contained an admission in the following sentence:

"Sometimes, John can be a little difficult to get along with."

The researchers showed the resumes to personnel

directors.

Can you guess which applicant the directors most wanted to interview?

Believe it or not, the answer is JOHN.

The conclusion made by the researchers was that John's resume was more likely to be real because it was more believable.

This example illustrates why you should let prospects know upfront what the weaknesses or limitations are of what you are offering. By doing this, you can accomplish several things:

First, by being upfront about the proper use of your product, service, or concept, your prospect will be less inclined to direct their focus on trying to uncover faults and weaknesses themselves. If someone is so focused on what the "catches" might be, it may divert their attention away from the positive benefits. If you get the damaging admissions out of the way first, you can shift them quickly to where you want them to focus.

Second, it lends credibility to everything else you have to say about your product or service. If you've been honest enough to admit the weaknesses and flaws of what you're offering, it will make logical sense for the reader to assume that all the positive things you have to say are real too. Selling something that isn't right for a customer doesn't make sense. You aspire to have happy, satisfied customers, right?

Third, it can capture a reader's attention. Who can resist a statement that begins with *"I shouldn't be telling you this, but...."*?

Cosmetics company Lush has long understood the power of the "damaging admission." Right alongside their product descriptions, they include positive and negative customer comments. Some are raving reviews - which a reader would expect. But a study that says *"smells a bit too earthy"* helps to refute the idea that the positive testimonials are not genuine, wouldn't you agree?

Many people are afraid of making damaging admissions because they think that by showing weakness, they'll lose a sale. In actuality, the opposite is usually the case. The fact is (and research shows) you're far more likely to win your customers' trust and respect if you admit flaws openly.

Opportunities to use damaging admissions can regularly appear in common questions customers ask you. You can also look at competitor reviews and forums to find common customer concerns.

You can also create damaging admissions, including a fixable solution from actual situations you have dealt with before. For example, you can add a story/case study of something that was an issue that the company resolved with a positive outcome. Postage and packaging problems are a great example e.g., *"My bottle of shampoo got cracked in transit, but the company replaced it quickly and gave me a bonus bottle as well, which was awesome!"*.

The example above is an excellent example of how you can show a reader what your company does in the circumstances you know people are worried about happening to them.

Don't be afraid of admitting faults. Instead, use these as a way to show what you did about it and what you learned. Your readers will appreciate your transparency.

Quoting Credible Sources

A third party statement is persuasive because it is directly self-evident or because it is independently verified by other sources. Especially useful are statements that are third party quotes from a historically credible source.

Name dropping and quoting well known third parties with established reputations shows:

1. You have done your homework

2. You have some alignment or inferred relationship with that source

3. Shows the high caliber of information you aim to share with your audience

Third-party endorsements are essential, especially for appeasing detail orientated readers and skeptics.

People who may have felt the need to leave your website to go check up on whether what you have been stating is factual may not feel the need to do so if you have included enough trackable, reliable data from outside sources.

Give readers everything they need from your content and control what they use for reference, and you will hold them to your page.

Bullets Are Your Friends

We already know readers have short attention spans. They want to assimilate information fast. An excellent way to help your reader get to the information they want fast is to offer information in bulleted lists.

Definition: A "bullet point" is an item introduced by a dot ("bullet") or a similar icon or numbered list style of bullets.

Bulleted lists are a helpful way to help skim readers quickly find the points that are of interest to them. They may also use the bullets to qualify the following content and to decide whether it is likely to contain the information they want. This may determine if they wish to keep reading.

Bullet points not only help your readers assimilate information, but they also help you to create concise but engaging, easy to absorb chunks of text.

Bullet points make it is possible to get important points across using a simple structure and punctuation.

Think of bullets as mini headlines. They should convey a clear benefit and promise to the reader. They encourage readers to skim through the content of your bullets, giving you the opportunity to entice them into reading further.

Bullets deliver text that is concise, easy to digest, useful, actionable, and to the point. Whoever provides the desired information first, wins in the content marketing game.

You can use bullets to capture attention by including topics that you know through your research are of the most interest. You can also use them to highlight any common issues or questions you know your readers have about the product or service you are writing about.

Use bullets like a table of contents, and assume your readers will be skim-reading them. They are essentially a teaser for the accompanying explanation you are going to include for each bullet in the paragraphs that follow.

Here are ten tips for creating easy to read, clear bullet points that highlight features, benefits, questions, concerns, steps, or suggestions.

Emphasize the beginning of the bullet with a concise

summary of the point you want to illustrate.

For example, if your bullets are questions, make sure all of the bullet points are questions and not statements mixed in with questions.

If you have more than one set of bullets on your page, you can have different genres or groups of bullets. For example, one set of bullets might be FAQs or a statement such as "*Top 5 tips to help you be better organized*".

Keep your bullet points symmetrical where possible. It's easier to read bullets that follow a consistent pattern of formatting, so your readers don't have to work hard to find what they are looking for. Keep your punctuation uniform. This means that if one bullet ends with a period (full stop), complete all points with a period.

Avoid ending bullet points with semicolons (;). This looks messy and is confusing.

Remember that bullets should be short and sweet, three lines maximum. Don't make your readers have to search and remember, it's a bullet point, not an essay.

Number bullet points when there are more than five, to help your readers stay on track, and avoid getting lost.

Don't use connecting words and phrases such as "secondly". These slow readers down and dilute the point you want to make.

Keep bullets thematically related. That is: ensure your bullet points are related to each other, especially if you have a lot of them. If there are more than 15, you may want to consider breaking them into more than one set unless they are highly related, and it makes sense to keep them together. Keep your punctuation and grammar uniform.

Be wary of using bullets points with sensitive or emotionally challenging material. If you do use them, you want to take a reader quickly to something that offers relief. For example, if listing a whole lot of negatives, you risk making people feel depressed to the point of turning them off. For emotionally charged content, you may be better off addressing each point one at a time with a subtitle and paragraph with a hint of a solution below it. Take care to take a reader to a solution quickly, so they get to feel better at every step. If you give them a positive dose at every level, they are much more likely to want to read on.

Maintain a clean layout. Avoid mixing fonts, sizes, or margin settings.

One of the best ways to make sense of an idea, especially online, is to break it down into digestible chunks.

Bullets points are like mini billboards, so use them effectively. Don't write boring bullets - give them meaning. For example, if you had recurring tonsillitis and were looking for a natural cure, which bullet point would you be more interested in:

Contains UMF honey from Kaikoura New Zealand OR

Contains soothing UMF honey with antibacterial & clinically proven healing properties to soothe a sore throat and fight bacteria

Add in a benefit if you can. How about this business

example:

- How to speak confidently in public

- How to talk with inner confidence & eliminate stage fright, whether you're a shy introvert or an outgoing extrovert!

Notice how the second one also solves a problem letting the reader know that if they are a shy person, it's not a big deal. Build curiosity and play on the mystery. Don't be afraid to add some mystique that a reader will want to explore further.

Create bullets from compound sentences to help you drive home a point while at the same time leveraging the usability of your content.

Use authority bullets where you quote third party research. These build curiosity and credibility at the same time. An example might be "Forbes magazine's 2015 research reveals that 7 out of 10 businesses...."

Cliffhanger bullets tease and hint at what's about to come. These are great for building anticipation of upcoming promotions, launches, or special events, live, or in content form.

Your bullets are like a giveaway sample at the store. Craft each bullet as if it were to serve as a mini headline. You can use a bullet point to give away a small sample that tempts and teases the reader into wanting more, or a further explanation.

Make sure your bullets offer something helpful. Make them useful, remedial, or solution orientated. You want to leave your readers feeling like they have gained something useful or valuable from engaging with your content. Most of all, you want to give readers hope and excitement - so they want to take another step, whether that be to get them to read more or a call to action if you want them to do something directly as a result of reading your bullet points.

Don't expect to achieve perfection with each and every bullet you write.

I do cover more tips for bullet writing in the chapter Guided Writing With Bullets (for when you're stuck with a case of writer's block), but you can refer to them for some ideas whenever you like.

Practice and keep practicing, so these principles become second nature, and in time you'll become a bullet point expert.

Call To Action Guidelines

The importance of congruency between a call to action text/button on a website with offsite content that links to those pages is frequently underestimated.

Designers become very focused on making a call to action graphic on a website attractive, so it fits into the overall design. Not enough attention goes into how the call to action ties in with the preceding pages linking to the site. When someone clicks a link or button, the user will have an expectation of what solution they might get when they land on the next page.

Creating a compelling call to action button comes down to a lot more than how it looks. This process of design is called UX copywriting.

A call to action is the connection or bridge between your content and where you want your readers to go next. Much effort goes into crafting compelling content, and so it makes sense to put just as much thought and care into crafting a compelling call to action in a link or button.

The Purpose of "Call to Action" Buttons

Call to action buttons can serve a variety of functions. The primary purpose of a call to action is to entice a visitor to do something. That something could be linking to another page, product, adding something to their shopping cart, downloading something, requesting information, signing up for a newsletter, or registering for a membership.

Types of "Calls to Action" buttons

There are many different types of call to action buttons. While each type aims to get visitors to perform a particular action, that action can vary considerably. Below are the most common types of call to action buttons (or they may be links):

1. Add to Cart Buttons

2. Download Buttons

3. Free Trial Buttons

4. Learn More Buttons

5. Sign Up Buttons

6. Biography Call To Action Buttons*

*A biography call to action button is one in which you add a third-party reference to yourself as an owner, expert, or teacher and state a call to action describing what the readers can get or use by visiting your website.

Of course, you don't or in many cases can't use to call to action buttons but rather text. Text call to action formatting in link form can be just as effective (if not more so) than graphics when placed in the right position amongst compelling related content.

When creating a call to action:

◆ Don't give your visitors an excuse to hesitate

◆ While urgency is necessary, tell the truth and make sure you are delivering what you promise at the next step (next page)

◆ Give them enough information in your call to action to decide to hit go and click

- Ask them to act NOW (give them an instruction)

- Be descriptive, describe a benefit, preferably with a *"without having to..."*

- Be concise and to the point

When writing call-to-action statements, it is best to include links within sentences. Over the years, I have found that a statement within a sentence will get clicked on more than a **click here** link.

Offer your readers something that is the next logical step to take next from what you just explained or outlined. Make sure it contains a directive with an explanation of what they are going to get.

For example, a link that states, *"To save up to 5 hours a week on your daily tasks, Claim your 14-day free trial now."* is more effective than "*Free trial **Click here**."*

Remember that if you include a reason and use the "do this to get that" formula, your response and click-through rates (CTR) will be higher. Your readers will feel like they are following the next natural step instead of being led to a sales pitch.

Continuity & Congruency

When you spend so much time building a rapport with your readers, it's imperative to keep continuity between what you are promising and what your readers get when they arrive at the destination you are sending them to.

In other words, whatever you promise your readers in your content, you need to deliver when they get to the place you are sending them. If you satisfy their expectations consistently, you'll build trust.

Amid a lot of different information, people are easily confused by links or buttons on one page that may offer one thing, but not deliver what they expect on the next page. The text you connect pages with is essential.

For example:

Let's say you tell someone in your content that they can get a FREE MEMBERSHIP, but the page they land on, after following your link button, says FREE REGISTRATION. They see different text and so then have to stop and think.

While this may not seem like a big deal, the slightly different language used means the reader has to pause for a moment to decide whether they can find and get what they want (and were promised).

Hesitation kills conversion.

People look for safety and consistency when they get asked to do something. Anything that seems slightly "off', or that makes them work can be enough to stop the flow and momentum towards the action you want them to take.

When you create content, try and use terms, colors, and anything else that people will recognize from the website or company branding. You can include catchphrases, terminology, images, product names, tag lines, and especially calls to action.

It's essential to use the same instructions and consistent wording of your offers. When you do this, you are building familiarity with your company's branding.

Readers will also find it easier to remember what you want them to do when they are ready to do it! You are preconditioning, training your readers what to expect from you, so make sure they feel like you are consistent!

What To Use For Content

This topic is a pretty easy one to cover. You should already have a swipe file with all of your customer questions and opinions about products and services.

When writing a book, I always use questions to create chapters because I know for sure my audience is curious about and interested in these matters.

If I add sections I know they are interested in, it helps me to be thorough when working my way through every topic they want to cover, what they need, and their potential issues.

Whether preparing to write books or writing blogs and other types of content, you can pick a topic, then write down a series of questions and answers that revolve around it.

Use your audience research to stimulate ideas & brainstorm content constructs.

List these in bullet form, then elaborate with a more

comprehensive description of each point below.

For example:

Bullet 1. (Question, step or statement)

Bullet 2.

Bullet 3.

Bullet 4.

Bullet 5.

Next, you can create paragraphs that go into more detail about each of these points.

Bullet 1.

Description of bullet point 1. Add solutions or steps etc.

And so on....

You can, of course, add pictures, graphs, or illustrations to break up your text.

Write stuff that makes people think or say, "WOW! I didn't

know that".

People love feeling awe-inspired and surprised (in a positive way). Tell inspiring stories within your content that are examples of happy and successful outcomes.

Article Example

The following is an example is an article I wrote that had over half a million views. Visitors to the website from the blog post converted to sales at a rate of 15% to 20%. Newsletter signups were high too.

See if you can spot the psychology behind each section of the article. Note that the writing isn't perfect - my English teacher would have covered it in plenty of red marks with suggestions for improvement, I'm sure. But it didn't need to be perfect - it just needed to relate to my audience, and it did!

Itchy Scalp Treatments: Using A Natural Home Remedy For Itchy Scalp Conditions

Yes, it can be extremely annoying and embarrassing having a scalp condition like dandruff, eczema, scalp infections, or a nasty itchy red rash on your scalp.

If you are suffering from:

- flaky itchy scalp, or do you have a dry scalp with redness and rashes that drive you crazy?

- scalp picking - do you constantly find yourself picking at & scratching your head?

- oily scalp and limp hair leaving you feeling less than your best

- embarrassing dandruff falling on your clothes

- or even a fungal infection of your scalp that can lead to lesions or scalp sores.

- hair falling out & patches on your scalp

Your instinct might be to pick up a product from the local store shelf or even your doctor. Most scalp treatments that promise relief from dry scalp conditions sound very attractive until you start reading the fine print.

Sodium Laureth or Lauryl Sulphate (SLS) What's that? Why do you have to call a Poison Control Center if you accidentally swallow shampoo? And what are those warning labels on the back all about?

What does it do to your scalp if it's that toxic?

Stop!

What you must know is that several chemicals, especially SLS, strip the natural oils from the skin and even corrode it, along with your eye membranes. Have you also noticed that your hair has been thinning? Well hair follicle damage is another little known but very common symptom of these chemicals.

Actually, most commercial shampoos & scalp treatments are designed to meet people's "sensory" expectations offering instant gratification and the illusion that they are doing their job. So therein lies the problem. For example adding silicone to conditioner induces an artificial shine but in truth can create problems long term including sensitivities.

Most people expect a shampoo to:

◆ Foam up nicely

◆ Smell good

◆ Take all the so-called "nasty" oiliness out of their hair

◆ Make their hair feel squeaky-clean

And that's a reasonable ask - think about it, if your shampoo didn't foam up, smell good, or leave your hair feeling squeaky-clean, would you trust it? Well, here's the thing: 90% of commercial shampoos achieve the foaming effect using the equivalent of engine degreasers to strip off not only dirt and grime but also valuable natural oils that your scalp needs.

Yes -your scalp needs natural oils. Without them, your body has no natural defence those oils are there for a reason! Your scalp needs to maintain a natural PH balance that if disturbed - can develop into a dry, itchy irritated scalp.

The good news is that there are many natural remedies you can use with moisturising oils and natural powerful alternatives to heal & reverse any scalp problem by restoring balance safely. You can easily repair follicle and damage - even boost hair growth and use your own home remedy for scalp cell regeneration.

There are also the artificial aromas that are added its alarming the huge percentage of people who are mild to severely averse or allergic to artificial scents and we don't even know it.

So what non toxic itchy scalp treatments and natural remedies can help?

Well there are many non toxic shampoos which are nourishing and conditioning while still giving you the "foam effect", they smell nice with the addition of the natural oils they contain. So you do have a choice and it does NOT have to cost you more, in fact most of them are less you just have to know what to look for.

So lets have a look at natural oils for treating your scalp:

Here are some of my favorite natural oils you can use for hair & scalp treatments.

Zinc Pyrithione: Wonderful stuff for scalp conditions. First synthesized in the 1930's, this is the most widely used active ingredient from a natural source. It's used to treat dandruff, seborrheic dermatitus, psoriasis, eczema and numerous other skin and scalp disorders. It has strong anti-fungal and anti-bacterial properties.

Jojoba: Is excellent as a scalp moisturiser and helps to rebalance sebum.

Tea Tree: Oily hair Treatment for dry scalp, dandruff, lice, and underactive sebaceous glands, enlivens the scalp and brings the cells & follicles to attention

Basil: Oily hair promotes growth

Chamomile: Fine to normal hair gives golden highlights

Clary sage: All types of hair dandruff treatment

Lavender: Normal hair Scalp treatment for itchiness, dandruff, and even lice!

Lemon: Oily hair Gives golden highlights; treatment for dry scalp, dandruff, lice, and underactive sebaceous glands

Myrrh: Dry hair Treatment for dry scalp, dandruff, lice, and underactive sebaceous glands

Patchouli: Oily hair Dandruff treatment

Peppermint: Dry hair Promotes hair growth

Rose: Fine hair Soothes scalp

Rosemary: Oily hair Dandruff treatment; promotes hair growth

Tea tree: Oily hair Treatment for dry scalp, dandruff, lice, and underactive sebaceous glands

Ylang-ylang: Oily hair Dandruff treatment

Neem: a wonder oil from India. Neem is amazing for all of the wonderful "stuff" it does. It's also derived from a type of tree bark. Neem is an effective fungicide and insecticide (great for head lice when used with geranium, rosemary, lavender and eucalyptus oils). In clinical studies Neem extracts and oil were found to be as effective as coal tar and cortisone in treating psoriasis with none of the usual side effects accompanying the use of Neem as there was with Coal tar and cortisone.

Neem extracts and oil removes redness and itching when

applied directly to your scalp and it's a great skin conditioner.

The best part of knowing that there are alternatives is the fact you can mix these into super powerful blends like a super moisture boosting home remedy for dry scalp, or soothing itchy scalp treatments yourself. Dry itchy scalp can be dealt with fast and permanently without spending a ton on traditional scalp med products.

Here's just one easy remedy you can make today:

Home remedy for dry itchy scalp Take c oatmeal and soak in water for 20 mins. Mix well and then strain the liquid adding it to a cup. Add 5 drops lavender oil (or lavender stalks steeped in cup hot water. Add 5 drops rosemary (or rosemary stalks steeped in cup hot water. Allow to cool until tepid.

Mix the liquids together and dab on your scalp, leave in for 10 mins to soothe the itch. This a good temporary soother for itching. Chamomile tea is also soothing!

There are hundreds of ideas that are excellent scalp treatments from dandruff to scalp infections like scalp sores & psoriasis. These remedies combined with the knowledge of what causes itchy scalp and other scalp conditions will enable you to be free from itching, dryness and allow you to grow fabulously thick, shiny beautiful hair also..so have fun experimenting and "luxuriating" by giving your hair a treat using the many natural gifts from nature that are right under our noses!

There are also many natural shampoos that so not use these ingredients and do wonders for your hair such as Akin shampoo, and Thursday Plantation which is fantastic as an effective anti-dandruff shampoo.

SOOTHING & HEALING ANTIFLAMMATORY REMEDY: Apply a mixture of 1 teaspoon of Neem oil (antifungal & antiitching) 1 teaspoon Teatree or Manuka (also antifungal) which much stronger than teatree, one teaspoon of Rosemary oil and one teaspoon of Lavender oil together in 3 tablespoons of carrier oils such as Olive or Almond oil (Wheatgerm and Macadamia carrier oils closely match your natural sebum) and apply to your scalp daily.

GARDEN REMEDY: Go to your garden and get 3 sprigs of Rosemary, and chop up and add to 3 tea bags of

Chamomile tea. Boil gently, let cool, strain and rinse your hair with this liquid for a calming anti-inflammatory effect.

There are many more remedies you can use to treat your scalp as well as many shampoos that are excellent value, contain no nasties to aggravate your scalp and hair follicles. It's really simple to treat yourself to your own pampering session and help heal your sore scalp. And then be kind to it by using only products that nourish your hair and scalp.... So have fun with oils and trying the remedies I mentioned above. You can have beautiful hair & healthy scalp when you know what is good for it – and what's not without spending a fortune and curing it yourself - naturally!

To find more natural scalp and skin remedies, as well as ready-made formulations you can buy and apply for scalp relief and shiny, healthy flake-free hair visit: www.website.com

End of article.

Can you spot the problems and questions addressed

here? I've appealed to their desire for a soothed calm scalp but also dealt with some issues they may not have been aware of before. The reason for doing this was to anchor them to the page, so they felt they had to read on to find out how to avoid those yucky chemicals and regain a healthy scalp.

(I used to have itchy scalp, so I was one of these people myself).

I gave them lots of useful explanations and remedies to use to show them I was sincere about helping them. They could read the natural remedies and check up on me to see whether they were credible recipes, too. Even though I was giving away my recipes, a significant proportion of people visited the website to buy the ready-made remedies and became regular customers.

Don't be scared to be generous! Help your audience and show them how helpful you are. If you are useful to people now, they may be curious and enthusiastic about learning what else you can deliver.

Graphic Design & Layout

The quality of images – or, more specifically, how professional they appear to be - can make or break your copy.

English speaking readers usually read from top left to bottom right. So the top left-hand corner of your page is "prime real estate."

The top left corner can be an excellent place to add a subscription box, but if you want your reader to read your content first, then avoid making this prime spot a distraction.

Use images carefully.

Here are 10 rules-of-thumb to follow for adding images:

Rule number 1 - don't use poor quality images EVER!

Rule number 2 - use two typeface families maximum. OK, maybe three.

Rule number 3 - pick colors purposefully. In other words,

pick colors that match your website or other content.

Rule number 4 - less is more, if you can use fewer images and still make the same point, then do it.

Rule number 5 - negative space is your friend. Don't be afraid of space around your content. It makes it more readable and highlights strong points you want to make.

Rule number 6 - don't be too cryptic.

Rule number 7 - symmetry is not your friend when it comes to content layout.

Rule number 8 - make it appeal to more than one type of reader and not just something that you personally like.

Rule number 9 - use consistent or complementary fonts

Keep your text font consistent or integral to the text on the rest of your page. Keep the shape and size of your images balanced.

Rule number 10 - use the rule of thirds. The rule of thirds is a "rule of thumb" or guideline which applies to the composition of visual images such as designs, films, paintings, and photographs.

The guideline proposes that an image should be imagined as divided into nine equal parts by two equally spaced horizontal lines and two equally-spaced vertical lines, and those critical compositional elements should be placed along these lines or at their intersections.

Make sure to keep your content clean. Too many images will distract the reader from the important points your text is making.

The Ultimate Copy Template

As many great copywriters have said, it's not necessary to be a prize-winning sales writer or English professor to create great sales content.

The fact is - writing good copy comes down to preparation and presentation of crucial points. Add your style and personality into the mix, while covering the essential features. The best copywriters I know all use templates to make the process of writing sales letters more efficient. Creating an audience-specific template also ensures all necessary points are covered.

What you see below is a 14 step sure-fire process to follow. This template is ideal for long copy, but you can still follow the same format for wiring other types of content - you may just need to condense it a little.

You may notice some deliberate reminders to jog your memory when writing using this template.

Overcoming Hurdles That Create Buying Resistance

Every reader will have some form of natural resistance to

being "sold to." It also presents an opportunity to connect with your readers. As you already know, the objective of your sales letter is to overcome your readers' buying resistance and encourage them to take the desired action.

Like an obstacle course, your sales letter leads your readers through a series of obstacles with an equal or higher number of rewards along the way. Any small win gives readers a taste of a BIGGER payoff at the end.

It doesn't matter what type of selling you are doing, be it verbal or written; you will encounter obstacles which are often in the form of questions such as:

"What if I can't do it, I'm not an expert."

"You don't understand my problem."

"How do I know you're qualified?"

"I don't believe you."

"I don't need it right now."

"It won't work for me."

"What happens if I don't like it?"

"I can't afford it."

Essentially, people arriving at your sales page who don't buy, fit into three categories:

- The "I don't want it" (and probably never did in the first place) person.

- Or the "I don't trust you or have enough confidence in what I see to buy yet."

- Or the "You haven't given me enough value to make a decision yet" (in this case, they might go shopping elsewhere).

Results-driven sales letters need to ensure that a reader has seen, heard, or felt enough positive reasons to proceed to the next step - to take the action you want them to take. If they haven't, they either don't want it, or you haven't yet done a good enough job of covering all the concerns a reader needs addresses to take another step.

The 14-step sales letter template is a system and format to help you overcome each of these objections in a precise, systematic way.

1. Grab a readers attention

2. Identify and relate to their possible reasons for wanting your stuff

3. Provide a solution

4. Build credibility

5. Demonstrate and explain the benefits of your product or service

6. Show social proof & third party endorsements

7. Justify and build confidence

8. Deal with their concerns and objections

9. Explain what you are offering

10. Give them a Shopping List

11. Include a guarantee or promise of service

12. Add a call to action and a why

13. Apply scarcity or other motivation for why they should take action NOW

14. Finish with a P.S. summarizing what they will get and remind them again why they need to act now.

These steps apply the carrot and stick mentality: attracting them to what they want and removing their pain in the process.

Motivation Is Emotional

Remember that people don't buy stuff based solely on logic; they buy because the stuff they want gives them a positive feeling or payoff. In other words, the logical justification behind the sale happens after they are emotionally engaged. So every step in the sales process must build on emotional reasons for buying, and be backed up with logical reasons too.

Remember the two things that motivate people (carrot

and the stick) - the promise of gain and the fear of loss. The stick - fear - is always the more significant motivator and has to be handled carefully.

Remember that people want to:

Feel popular and included

Feel abundant (or wealthy)

Feel attractive

Feel healthy

Feel secure

Feel peaceful and happy

Have more time

Have fun

Because they want to meet the human needs of:

Certainty and Security

Uncertainty or Variety

Feeling Significant or Important

Feeling Connected or Loved by Someone

Growth and Contribution

Contribution to the Whole (all of humanity)

These "payoffs" are what your readers **really** want. What you are selling is just a conduit for fulfilling these needs in some way.

The 14 Step Copy Writing System

Now that we've covered what makes people tick when buying a product or service let's get into the nitty-gritty of content creation.

* * *

1. Grab Attention

Titles and sub-headlines are your first opportunity to capture attention. If the reader likes your title, they may decide to skim read through the rest of your page.

Remember to use descriptive words and include a benefit (carrot) plus a way for them to avoid pain (stick).

"How to do _____ without having to do _____"

2. Identify And Relate Through The Problem

Now that you have captured your reader's attention, you need to identify any issues they may be having and determine how they may be feeling about them. Write about what other people like them who are dealing with these same issues are saying. The idea is that your readers feel they can identify with the concerns and think, "Yeah, that's my problem and how I feel, too.", or "These people sound like they are dealing with the same issues as me." Next, you need to exaggerate the issues so your readers feel them more acutely.

In copywriting speak this technique is commonly referred

to as; "problem - agitate." Poke and prod the sore spot to remind a reader that the issue is indeed a major pain in the butt for them. Pain and discomfort are strong motivators, so you have to push a reader into their pain zone to the point of realization that they want help.

When writing a sales letter, you can be bolder when pushing buttons. When writing a blog or other content, you can do this gently and talk about the painful thing, or what someone is missing, in a more subtle way.

You can talk about potential consequences and also introduce stories or examples of people with similar issues having solved them.

Build on the concern, but not so much as to make them feel too awful to the point they lose faith.

3. Provide A Solution

Now that you've captured your readers' interest by highlighting their issue and reminding them how it's causing them pain or irritation, you can lead them towards a solution.

This is where you begin to educate your reader about the solution. Build interest and also credibility; you can do this by telling stories or offering examples.

4. Build Credibility

Now it's time to explain who you are and why your reader should believe you. Why?

Well, your reader doesn't know you yet, so why should they believe what you say? Give them a solid basis for trusting your statements by including social proof.

At this point, you can work on building on that foundation by talking specifically about your experience and introducing any of the following:

1. Your significant awards and/or recognitions

2. How long you've been practicing your field of expertise

3. Conferences at which you've been a guest speaker

4. Successful case studies

5. A damaging admission that shows you've made, and

learned from, your mistakes

6. Prestigious names you have worked with or done business with

This shows that you've done the hard yards and made the mistakes to earn credibility. It also shows your readers that you have the knowledge and expertise to show them what they need to do to achieve the results they're looking for.

Add a "damaging admission." If you have made any significant mistakes that are embarrassing or silly, but (and here is the critical part), talk about the valuable and/or priceless lessons you learned as a result.

If you are feeling anxious about doing this at this point, that's ok - just remember that people are more trusting of someone more who is willing to say, *"Hey, I'm not perfect, and I don't pretend to be."* Your readers are likely to want to hear about your mistakes, so they can avoid them. Remember, if you are prepared to step out on a limb and talk about your imperfections, your credibility will increase.

If you've made a genuine mistake - and we all have - share

it!

An excellent example of turning around so-called failures into positives is illustrated by Thomas Edison's reply when he was asked "*How did it feel to fail 1,000 times before you invented the lightbulb?*" His famous answer was "*I didn't fail 1,000 times. It was just a 1,000 step process.*"

Like Mr. Edison, emphasize the benefits of your mistakes and reframe them as a valuable learning curve with a positive benefit.

Make your mistakes all about your reader, and how they can avoid having to go through the 1000 steps you did before they succeed!

5. Demonstrate and Explain The Benefits

Here is where you put your teacher's hat on and show your audience how they can use what you are offering them to get what they want. Remember: people want to feel a particular way; they want to know what the thing or service they are buying can do for them. And they want to know this far more than what color something is or what fancy technology something has.

Talk about the features of a product or service briefly (without being too wordy), then spend much more time talking about how they can get to their desired result.

The _____ has _____ and _____ so you can do [insert all the things they want to have and feel as a result of buying the _____].

Let's digress for a moment. Grab a piece of paper and draw a line down the center and jot down all the features your product or service offers on the left-hand side. Now think about all the benefits of each point and write down all of the ways those features and benefits can fulfill their wants on the right.

Let's say you are selling a new type of range extender for cell phones with the latest breakthrough technology in iridium crystals. You might mention how the Rangeextender 5000 has the latest iridium crystal technology. More importantly, is HOW fancy iridium blue crystals increase a mobile phone range by over 450% so they can enjoy that fishing or skiing trip and for the first time, be contactable if they need to take calls from the office.

Think about obvious benefits and then extend them to how these benefits will make your reader FEEL. How will those benefits make their life better?

Use the IF, THEN, WITHOUT format, for example: "If you do this, then you can have [insert the thing they want], without having to[insert pain that is usually associated with doing or getting what they want]."

You can use bullet points if you wish to make the text easier to read and highlight several positive aspects of your product or service.

6. Offer social proof & third party endorsements.

At this point, the readers' logical side usually starts to make an appearance. Testimonials and third party endorsements from associates can be added at this point to back up what you say and provide further evidence of your credibility. Use case studies or anything else to show you are who you say you are and can deliver what you promise.

7. Provide justification and build confidence.

However much someone wants something, at some point, usually, when they are about to pull out their credit card to pay for it - they look for logical reasons to justify their purchase. Have you ever watched n L'Oreal ad and noticed that right at the end of the ad, the model always says, *"Because you're worth it"*? Because the company knows that women sometimes feel like makeup is a luxury, they might not feel they deserve it. It's is a powerful way to say, *"you should feel good about buying our makeup."* It's a very clever ad!

Help your readers justify their purchase:

You can give them value-based reasons why it's worth it

Personal satisfaction based reasons

Even peer associated rewards such as *"your staff/wife/ friends will really appreciate it."*

You should also make sure they believe they can achieve

what you are proposing. If your service is something that involves training, skill, or self-discipline, you must make sure your reader feels like they can achieve it.

They may be thinking that they are not famous enough, skilled enough, smart enough, or have failed before. There may be a myriad of reasons they might lack confidence in themselves or in anyone's ability to help them achieve their goal.

To accomplish this, you could refer to other people who have had similar experiences before, but then add a point of difference to explain why and how they overcame those obstacles and succeeded by taking a different approach. Explain or show that you understand the reasons WHY they have not managed to get to what they wanted before, and why it is possible now.

The point is, you have to help them feel they can do or be what they need to so they can get what they want.

Give them a reason to talk themselves into thinking the decision to buy is not only a good one from a feel-good point of view, but also why it's possible to achieve and why it also makes financial sense.

Make it easy for them to check all boxes they need to check in their mind in order to make a purchase.

8. Deal with concerns.

When purchasing something, almost everyone has questions and concerns they need answered. The last thing you want is for someone to leave your page because you didn't answer a question for them.

Pull out all of the questions and concerns you uncovered from your research. By focusing on primary concerns and including a few frequently asked questions you know your audience will be wanting to know the answers to, you are doing several things:

◆ You are confirming that you understand their concerns

◆ You are inferring or stating that you have taken care of the things that they are afraid of happening to them

◆ You are validating the people that think theirs might be a silly question

◆ Other people have had these concerns too, yet buying your product or service worked out very well for them without those concerns being a problem

◆ You are confirming your commitment to addressing and solving your readers' concerns moving forward

Take the opportunity to connect with your readers again and reassure them that you understand what they need and can help them.

9. Explain what you're offering

Your offer is one of the most important parts of your sales letter. It needs to wow the audience with an attractive combination of price, terms, and bonuses (if any).

Now is the time to talk about everything your reader will get when they buy your product or service. Give them a rundown of everything in bullet points, then explain each point in further detail. Offer plenty of extras if appropriate to raise the perceived value of your offer.

Be clear and concise. You can get to the point in this section because you've done the groundwork to prepare for this moment – the part where you present your offer.

10. Shopping list

Remember that in the T.V. salesperson example, I talked about the shopping list. Add a list of must-haves for anyone who wants the best _____. Give your readers a list of things they need to look for in a product or service to ensure they are getting the best value, quality, or whatever you want to emphasize.

Add your unique list of essentials for anyone who may decide to go elsewhere and compare offers from competitors. You can introduce your unique selling propositions (USPs). Highlight the relevance of these points and their benefits compared to the competition.

11. Insert a guarantee or promise of service

To lower the risk, you can offer a guarantee or a free trial. If you are not able to offer a money-back guarantee, you can emphasize your commitment to customer service and explain how you respond to customer inquiries. It's very important to clarify your guarantee and customer service policy, so readers know what to expect if something goes wrong.

Give the strongest guarantee you can afford to offer.

12. Provide scarcity or other motivation to take action NOW

Even if your offer is intriguing, if a reader has no reason to act now, they won't be compelled to make an immediate decision. It could be because their problem is not troubling enough to deal with immediately, it could be they are waiting for funds, they may plan to shop around, or they could just be thinking they will come back later when they are ready to buy.

Most of the time, people need some extra incentive as motivation to buy now. Help them jump that hurdle through scarcity.

You can create urgency by offering a limited number of products, services, or memberships. You can add a time limit, or just take the whole offer off the table on a specific date.

Whatever you decide to put in place as your point of

urgency, make sure you stick to it. If you say a discount finishes on a specific day or time, follow through with that and end it when you say you will. If you don't, you will lose credibility and train your audience that there is no urgency.

13. Add a call to action and a reason to act now.

Your readers have come a long way so far. They understand what your offer is about and what to expect. Now you need to tell them what to do next. Ask them to take action.

"Start here". Lead your reader to the next step. Some people feel bossy telling people what to do so directly, but just like walking a customer to the front of a store to make a purchase, it's polite and helpful to guide your audience to the next step. It's just common courtesy to show them where to go next and not leave them hanging trying to decide what to do.

If you are writing a blog post, you can tell them where to find more information or where to buy something you have referenced in the post. Alternatively, you can add a call to action in your bio if adding your content to another parties' blog.

Your bio should include a small statement about your self or the company and include a hook connecting that with what a reader wants.

You can add a promise of more of what they want, rather than necessarily a "buy this now" type call to action. "Learn more about how to _____" is an obvious and common example. Or Mia Gordon teaches people how to _____ without having to do _____.

Add something that intrigues them and draws them in to want to learn more, or ask them to take action directly if you're writing a sales letter.

14. Finish with a P.S. summarizing what they get and why they need to act now

You may be surprised to learn that the postscript, the P.S. - at the end of your content, is one of the most important parts of a sales letter, according to top copywriters.

Your reader has had a lot to assimilate: By the time they

have gotten to the bottom of the page, they may have forgotten some of the reasons why buying your stuff is a good idea. It's important to summarize what they'll get and offer a reminder of why it makes sense to buy. It helps your reader consolidate their desires, and move them past any last minute hesitation.

Remind them of why they need to act now, and exactly what to do. Again, you need to be clear, concise, and direct about to do next.

So that's it - you're almost done! Well – nearly. Let your content piece sit for a day and then go back over it. A next day proofreading session will help you refine your content down to a polished finished product, and you'll find all those little typos you could have sworn you'd already fixed the day before.

I admit punctuation is not my strong point, and because I'm a speed reader, I often miss connecting word errors even if I'm proofreading content days later.

Here are some tips to keep handy when writing copy:

Don't be too much of a perfectionist. As long as your basic

punctuation and spelling are good, and you speak to the people who your content is most relevant to. They will be much more interested in how well you understand what they want and need than in your technical skill as a writer.

Use your research to come up with features and benefits. Keep these notes handy at all times, and keep relating them to the desired outcome of your reader.

Keep a log of any good ideas you have when writing. That way, you can develop a swipe-file of winning phrases.

Keep your sentences and paragraphs short, and avoid sentences that require lots of commas. The idea is to write in a style that is clear and easy-to-understand, even for a reader who is in a hurry.

Don't worry about the length of your copy. The longer copy article is statistically proven to be beneficial for high search engine ranking; Google loves long copy provided it's helpful and instructive.

Research proves readers don't mind long copy either as long as it's skimmable and contains information that is relevant to them. If your layout is clear and formatted with clear titles, they should be able to find what they are looking for.

Don't be afraid of white space. Leave plenty of space around your text to emphasize your text.

Use bold, italics, and underline to emphasize important points. You can also use highlighting, albeit sparingly.

Next, I'm going to cover some a few tips for how to layout your content for different goals.

Print Ads

Print media is a tricky medium to master. It needs to show a condensed combination of key points that hook your readers' attention & make them want to take action.

You usually have only a very small space to work with, so make it effective.

Use the AIDA principle:

AIDA principle (*Attention, Interest, Desire, Action*) is an acronym for a principle coined by the American sales and advertisement legend Elias St. Elmo Lewis in the late 1880s. The principle consists of four key stages in the advertising process: obtaining the attention of a potential customer, evoking interest in a product or a service, developing the desire in the customer to have what is offered, and inducing action which might lead towards the purchase. The AIDA principle is no longer used as an exclusive marketing approach, but it is still an important part of advertising.

Make your images count. Unless they have a message or purpose or a logo, think carefully about how much they contribute to your content. If they are confusing, people grow focused on trying to work out what the image means, at which point you will have lost the impact.

Offer an eye-catching benefit, how people can get or achieve [insert thing they want] so they can [insert final desire and what they want to feel] without having to do [insert thing they hate most and want to avoid].

Give them succinct reasons why they would want XYZ.

Add a strong call to action right at the bottom of the page.

These are pretty much the main ingredients in a good print ad.

Article & Blog Specific Formatting

I'm sure you agree, writing excellent articles that address niche market problems is one of the most potent and effective ways to build inbound links and drive qualified traffic to a website.

To recap: When people read a blog post, they generally expect one or more of the following things:

- To be entertained

- To be given information to help them make a decision

- To help them solve a problem

- To be educated and informed

- To be taught how to do something

- To feel something as a result of reading the post

- To solidify something they already know, but want further confirmation on

Your job, therefore, as a writer, is to uncover your readers' intent and what is most likely to give them satisfaction in your content.

You can break blog posts down into a series of subjects where you cover all of the points that your audience wants to know.

If you have done your homework correctly, you should already have a list of points they want to be covered. As I keep reiterating, many times, you can take them through a series of steps starting with identification and qualification, then moving on to building trust and association.

At the end of the page, you can summarize what they learned, why they can safely make a decision based on this information, and what to do next.

Because blog posts are the most common type of content to write, I want to include a format specifically for articles, plus cover how to write a compelling bio.

Articles can be about resources, how-tos, solving a problem, teaching something, or addressing an issue, and they're easy to write when you use this simple template:

1. Write a headline that points out a problem and contains your primary key phrase, for example: "How to break a bad habit in 5 days."

2. Add a quick Summary (and include a relevant secondary key phrase). This summary should be only one paragraph, 3-5 short, concise sentences summarizing the content of your article.

3. Use your first paragraph after the abstract (summary) to point out how the problem or concern might impact them.

Try to include your primary key phrase or a variant of it for relevance. Elaborate on the problem and highlight it to make it more apparent. Explain the ways this problem can impact them.

4. Offer solutions outlined in bullet format.

Next, suggest a few examples of how the reader can solve the problem or improve their situation.

5. Summarize: close on a positive note.

End your article with a paragraph or two that summarizes your most important points. Wrap up with a positive spin that gives them hope and something positive to move toward.

6. Include your contact info - your bio information. You have built your readers' interest and desire. They are hopefully feeling positive about the concepts and ideas you have given and so will likely want to contact you for more information, services, or products. Many websites (if not your own) will allow you to include four to six lines that provide your contact information and even a plug for your latest product or service.

How to create a good bio summary:

Write your bio as a third-party description of who you are and what you offer.

1) Include your name (you want to brand yourself!)

2) Include your site name (your domain name or URL)

3) Include a relevant keyword as anchor text e.g., Mia Gordon, author, and founder of http://

www.mywebsite.com has helped hundreds of itchy scalp sufferers overcome dandruff and other scalp conditions. On www.mywebsite.com/page, you can download information about scalp remedies, plus tips and information about how to relieve annoying scalp itch fast! Keyword proximity is important so use keyword-rich sentences

4) A bio should be 2-3 sentences long

5) Add a USP if you can.

This format is a shortened version of the content template and works well for blogs that need to be shorter.

Social Media

Social media can be fun even for introverts like me. The thing I like about Social Media is that it's possible to get away with being a little bit cheeky and inject some humor - if you're careful with this as we've all seen this backfire when overdone!

A lot of people post random stuff on Social Media without purpose. It's fun to do this outside of work, but when it comes to sending traffic to your website, it is crucial to post with a clear intention. Even if you are not directly trying to sell something through a post (not posting any more than 30% commercial posts a day), you can still tie in statements that engage the reader with something relevant to their interests.

You can build a linked series of posts that explain something or cover common concerns in a helpful way.

Tips:

Use keywords and decent length descriptions of 200 to 300 words. Posts with links to them from social media are more likely to be indexed by search engines faster.

Give credit where possible to others, especially to authority sites and brands, which lends added credibility to your brand.

Statistics show that people love to experience surprise and awe on social media. Give them something to shift them away from their standard patterns of thinking. That's why awesome photos and videos go viral.

Demonstrate, help, teach!

Show photos of other people doing what your audience wants to do in their language!

And of course answer questions. Let your audience get to know you, share your expertise by answering questions online and helping them everywhere you can on social media.

Social Checklist

Aim for viral spread of your own and preferably customer photos using keyword detailed descriptions and searchable #hashtags.

High-quality photos and videos that have well-researched keyword content based on popular or trending topics. Use #hashtags.

Use Google Analytics converting keyword phrases to search for trending topics. Google Trends is another good source of keywords.

Choose high-quality photos that include:

- Fun

- Awe

- Curiosity

- Fascination

- Images – good quality pictures and videos

- Add # hashtags

- Add URL if uploading image from computer

- Comment on other posts

Use statements, including phrases like:

- How to

- Why people

- You could

- If you

- Ways to

- Top reasons to

- Tops reasons why

- Why it's

- Things to consider

- The crucial point to remember is

Post comments on related accounts.

Remember to include the essential points for your

audience and topic, and to be helpful and knowledgeable at the same time.

Add:

- Images – good quality pictures and videos

- Add # hashtags

- Add URL where appropriate

- Comment on other entities posts

- Contribute to other peoples' pages with helpful, relevant content

Use statements, including phrases like:

- How to

- Why people

- You could

- If you

- Ways to

- Top reasons to

- Tops reasons why

- Why it's

- Things to consider

- Important things to remember

With all social media, remember to include the essential points for your audience and topic and to be helpful and knowledgeable.

Firstly, use keyword and intent-based combinations of phrases in your titles.

Secondly, use the precise and correct formatting of your posts' content. If linking to a page, use a sufficient number of words to make your post highly relevant to the page to which it links. If not linking to a page and creating an image post, make sure that the description is a decent length to make it more searchable in Google and other search engines.

Using templates makes it much easier to write content your audience will love.

Contain "hooks" to relate your content to your audience's interests and desires. Relate their needs and wants to what you have to offer, deliver value to prospects, and lead them to the desired action as part of your sales funnel. Remember that your offsite content IS part of your sales funnels!

Use up to 5 hashtags, and include some that relate to the main generic topic, plus some that interlink between other posts. Make sure your hashtags are highly relevant to the post, reinforcing your credibility, and so hashtags that get clicked will bring up posts that have synergy with the connecting topics.

Plan out your posts. One in 4 to 5 posts should be about a product or service you promote. Give your audience something of value in each post, such as a post, even if it's small.

Use non-product and service promotion posts to educate

the reader, so when you do promote posts about "your stuff," you don't have to try to throw all the features and benefits into one post.

Write five posts leading up to the "sales post" that talks about the benefits of your product or service.

Entertain your audience while TEACHING them that you are the expert and that there is a history behind your product or service.

Construct your descriptions using our who, what, why, where, when, how, questions to think of engaging ideas for posts.

Part Six

Optimising For Search Engines

Search engine optimization has changed and expanded immensely in the last few years! But there are still fundamentals writers can learn about how SEO relates to content writing, and how to format your content so search engines can easily find and read your content.

One upon a time SEO was pretty much all about:

1. The number and relevance of links to your pages

2. Site structure and navigation

3. On-page optimization of your content

Current search engine optimization is all about:

1. The number and relevance of links to your pages (even more important)

2. Site structure and navigation

3. On-page optimization of your content

4. Bounce rate on website

5. Engagement & number of pages visitors view

6. Number of authority connections via social media or links (how many authority sites or personal profiles are pointing to the website)

7. Semantic search

8. Mobile optimization

What this means is that Google and other search engines use many more indicators to evaluate a website page's importance. They pay attention to which websites high authority website link out to, and how well those landing pages satisfy visitors. They determine this by assessing which authority sites are linking to the site and by looking at visitors' behavior onsite, such as bounce rate and time on site, through analytics.

What can you do to make your page more authoritative and search engine friendly?

Well, the longer your page is, offering steps, facts, charts, images, and adequately formatted alt text descriptions with clearly visible titles (H1, H2, etc.) tags, the higher it is likely to rank. Your page also needs to have both a meta and H1 title that contains your main keywords.

The importance of adding keywords to your title may be evident. Still, the text that follows your headers, and the relevance of any subtitles to your main title, also help Google's' semantic algorithms to determine the context of each paragraph and, therefore, the whole article.

Make it easy for search engines to ascertain all of the useful content on your pages. If that content holds visitors onsite for longer then other websites' pages and has authority (links, shares, for example), it is more likely to rank well.

Pages with easy to read, resource-rich content tend to

rank well.

When you add images, look for the option to add 'alt text,' add keywords that are relevant to both the image alt text and the keywords in your titles. Google can read images, so be accurate about describing what your pictures are, and you'll enhance the searchability of your photographs.

Use H1, H2, H3, H4 tags. Surround title and bold text with other relevant text that gives context to those titles. For example: let's say the title of your article was 'How To Repair Cells At Home.' Google only knows what type of cell you are referring to from the surrounding text on the page. Are you talking about human body cells? Are you talking about battery cells? Maybe you are talking about cell phones.

The only way search engines know what you are referring to is through semantic indexing of your pages. The algorithm references images, subtitles, and surrounding text to determine the context of the page. The relationship between different elements on the page tells Google and other search engines how the content is useful for the search intent. So the more clues you can give the search engine robots that crawl your page, the higher the likelihood of your pages ranking well.

Link back to your page from content that also has high relevance to your page. Use hashtags and descriptions that closely relate to your page. Help search engines identify your page as 'popular' amongst the websites which are most relevant or authoritative.

If your page holds visitors' attention and satisfies them, you have achieved your goal of optimizing your page.

Promoting Your Content

Social media, linking, ads, email are all ways you can promote your page.

Again, work on quality, not quantity. Think relevance, not numbers! Semantic search wants to see connections made with your page by other relevant external sources.Â

When you create content for social media or any other promotional material, here are some guidelines to follow:

Make the content you post highly relevant to the article/page where you are sending visitors. Create a mini version of the article using similar keywords and hashtags. Use images that relate to your page as well.

- When encouraging likes and shares, comment on similar posts that have been posted by authoritative sites.

- Try to find many people influential people and websites to acknowledge your post.

- Create bios in the third party, as a description of

yourself, and add an enticing call to action with it.

Part Seven

Causes & Cures For Writers Block

Writer's block is a creativity killer that writers all encounter from time to time. I'm covering it here because it's something that needn't paralyze you when it strikes.

Writer's block can last for days or even months. I used to have long periods of intermittent writer's block. I thought I was suffering from a lack of inspiration, a lack of motivation, and a creative black hole. Sound familiar? What it was for me was just fear and lack of self-confidence, it is for most people, you can easily overcome it.

When you are feeling discouraged about your writing, it's easy to use this as an excuse to give up writing or drive yourself buts trying to force yourself to write. The good news is that it's also common to have a sudden resurgence of enthusiasm if you can let go of your expectations and give your writing bug a little help to kick it back into gear.

Some of the most common causes of writer's block are:

- Fear of judgment and lack of confidence

- Fear of failure

- Burnout

- Perfectionism

Let's delve a little deeper into these issues and talk about some habits & belief systems that you can implement to help you move past them.

If you take a look at these descriptions, you may have noticed that they are all fundamentally based on fear.

"I cannot give you the formula for success, but I can give you the formula for failure--which is: Try to please everybody." Herbert Swope

Let's take a look at these fears:

Sometimes we have unreasonable expectations of ourselves to try to write a masterpiece. We think it's essential to appear intelligent, authoritative, witty, or enchanting, perhaps. What we need to remember is that people don't care how funny or technically savvy you are, they are reading your text to get an emotional fix from it of some kind.

You don't need to be perfect to write engaging content! So next time you are mentally beating yourself up - give yourself a break!

Complexity is not necessarily better either when what your reader is looking for is someone who can solve their problem & deliver a solution to their needs. They want you to be clear and concise; this is usually true. If you add embellishments and humor, that's great, but if you look at the content that gets shared the most, you will notice the focus is on how helpful and credible it is, not the author's technical writing skill.

So, once again, go back to your reader research and the

profiles you created as part of your original homework. Write down what they most want or want to avoid, then run through the title ideas page to brainstorm some ideas. Once you've established a concept, then break it down into bullet points - like a mini list of contents to follow. Then start writing in small chunks. You'll be surprised how these small steps can stimulate a flow, and next thing you know, you're coming up with plenty of stuff to write.

Fear of failure and perfectionism. I suffered from those afflictions for years, so I know they can be debilitating. I have learned to let myself off the hook and give myself a break. By taking the pressure off and not allowing self-criticism to take hold, it becomes easier to let creative energy to flow.

Burnout. A lack of motivation and inspiration from mental exhaustion is what writers complain of most often. When you have run out of ideas and enthusiasm, it can feel daunting thinking you need to force yourself to come up with material.

It's much easier to go back to the chunking method at this point. Rather than try to be creative, approach it from a technical point of view. Just add the paragraph titles or bullets as an outline. Aim to come back to each paragraph to fill in the details later. This exercise, in itself, can free your creative vision.

Creative beliefs – a significant hindrance to writing is the belief that some people have got writer's talent others haven't. Talent is part of it, yes, but if you enjoy writing, there is a high likelihood that your dormant ability is sitting there waiting for the right catalyst to bring it to life.

Shoulding on yourself. Telling yourself, "I should be this" or "I should have done that instead of this." Being a perfectionist can paralyze you, so start small and keep adding to your page, one paragraph at a time. You can always go back and tidy up your content later with a fresh mind.

One of the things I have learned about content writing is that going back to something you wrote earlier, and turn that raw content into something makes sense, that connects with your readers and their desires.

Your belief in your ability can come from the fact that you

can, and are able to learn this stuff. And it's really not that hard when you have the understanding and the system to go with it. So be kind to yourself when you have writer's block and have faith that the inspiration to add the finishing touches will come later.

The following tips will help you to get started when a bout of writer's block has frozen you :-)

* * *

Write Your Headline First

Starting with your headline gives you an anchor, a starting point.

Remember that headlines are an advertisement for the rest of your content. Your headline should describe how your content will solve an issue - and get your readers closer to their desired outcome.

Here are some concept headlines to stimulate ideas:

4 Stages of X

Checklist (to help achieve _____)

Common or Obscure Problems & Solutions

Controversial Opinion About Something

Why I Don't Believe In _____

Current & Topical Events

Euphemisms

Goal Setting - How To Achieve _____

Golden Rules For Doing Something

Grateful For

Holiday Ideas For

How To Do Something

Thing I Love About

Industry Trends

Laws of X

Location Based Title (how to do _____ in _____)

Ways To Save X

Mistakes To Avoid

Motivational Triggers

Myth Busting

Newspaper Style Title

Overcoming Objections To Common

Pain Avoidance, How To Avoid

Personal Story About Something

Predictions For Something

Product Review

Pros and Cons Of

What I Leaned From

How To Save Time/Money

Secrets Of

The Perfect Cure For

The Uncommon and the Unusual Ways To

Things I've Learned From

Things To Do

Things to Avoid

Timeline or History of X

Top 7 Tips

Traditions Of Successful

How To Escape From

Victory & Overcoming X

Hove To _____ In [#] Easy Steps

How To _____

How To Find

How To Rock

How To Make A Strong

How To Completely Change

How To (route That Gets)

How To Use _____ To Stand Out

How To Create _____ The Right Way

X Inspirational Ideas For

What To Do With

Where To Find

Quick Guide To

A Complete Guide To

Ultimate Guide

Beginners Guide

Hack

DIY

The Anatomy of _____ To Get

Things your _____ Doesn't Tell You

Trends For [YEAR]

EX Things Every _____ Should

X Amazing _____ To Try Right Now

Insane _____ That Will Give You

Types Of

Questions You Should Ask Before

Secrets To

Resources to Help You Become

Signs You Might

Point Checklist

Rules For

Habits of

Ideas To

Trends You Need To Know

Best _____ To

Why We love

Facts About

Essential Things For

Key Benefits Of

Examples Of _____ To Inspire You

Ideas That Will Motivate You Achieve

Reasons _____ Doesn't Work

Working Smart With

Smart Strategies To

Most Effective Tactics To

Mast Popular Ways To

Essential Steps To

Wrong Ways To

Creative Ways

Tips For Busy

No Nonsense

Surprising

Foolproof Tips For

Epic Formula To

Handy Tips From _____ To

Superb Ways To _____ Without

Tricks To

Ways To Make Sure Your _____ Is Not

Mistakes You'll Never Make Again

Weird But Effective Ways To

Super Tips That Will Make You

Supercharge Your

Pleasant Ways To

Wittiest _____ To

What No One Tells You About

Guided Writing With Bullets
Recap on the benefits of bullet points:

- They draw immediate attention to a section of the page you want people to pay attention to.

- They help to qualify your content quickly for skim readers whose eyes are searching for anchor points on the page as an indicator that the content on your offer is relevant and of interest to them.

- They help you to break your content down into easy to manage chunks. Like a Table of Contents, you can list your most important points through bullets to capture a reader's attention, then elaborate on each bullet point with a paragraph or two explaining the point further.

- Bullet points also help you as a writer to cover a series of important messages you want to convey.

- You can use them to relate to your readers by touching on any concerns, or by building on their desires.

For example:

Concern Bullets

Top 5 Concerns Consumers have when buying an XYZ.

1. Value: explain why this is a valid concern

2. Fit/Sizing

3. Guarantee

4. Which model

5. Upgrade capability

These points are a very general summary of what someone might be concerned about, and I'm sure you could come up with some points that relate to your products or services.

Concern-based bullet points tell readers that A) you understand their issues and B) you are setting the scene for their assumption that you will be offering a solution and C) they are validated in their concerns, and they are not silly. This combination gives them hope and even a little relief that if they read on, you will help them through a resolution to their concerns.

Step Bullets

5 Important Steps To _____ A Successful _____

1 Homework: add a hook or something they may not have known

2 Preparation:

3 Presentation:

4 Must have elements 97% of _____'s forget

5 Finishing tricks to make your _____ exceptional & outstanding

Step bullets offer a compelling opportunity to demonstrate your products or highlight the company's unique benefits and get your prospects excited.

You can build in some mystery, so they feel excited or

curious about learning something new. Here is your opportunity to stand out from the crowd.

Things To Avoid: Bullets and other Bullet Point ideas:

3 Things To Avoid When _____

6 things I learned about _____

Top questions experts get asked about _____

Smart questions people ask about _____

7 Ways To _____

Little Known Tips To Improve Your _____

Refer to your headline examples for more ideas.

Bullet points help to focus your readers' immediate attention. They also make your content easier to follow and for readers to find what they are seeking. Bullet points can and should lead readers from one point to the next, whetting their curiosity and tempting them to read on.

Use bullet points to connect with your readers, offer a clue that you have valuable information to share, so they want to engage further with the rest of your content.

Chunking

Break your content down into manageable sized chunks. Within each piece come up with a problem, the reader may want to solve, such as finding something, fixing something, saving time on something, saving money etcetera.

Follow this pattern to help you come up with content:

- Engage, identify and relate

- Build on your point, make them feel safe and that any concerns they have are valid or shared by others like them

- Point out steps for how to solve an issue or get closer to a goal

- Validate and prove why this works or why they should believe you

- Suggest an action

Start by building the inner core of your content; then, you

can pull each segment together in a flowing sequence.

PART EIGHT

Final Words

In my years as an online marketer since 2003, there are several things that stand out as the most important principles to adhere to as a content writer. One of these is to focus on creating quality versus quantity of content.

The first thing I learned was that the amount of success I achieved is **always** directly related to the amount of value I delivered to my audience. How much value I could provide was always determined by the amount of research I did on an audience before starting.

Learning what my audience loves, hates, talks about, and, most importantly, staying focused on how they want to FEEL throughout the whole process was the key to staying on point.

I have found that writing content systematically, then placing it on websites that attract the right kind of readers, is key to attracting higher converting referral traffic to my websites. I don't bother writing content for people that aren't my target market or who are "fringe audiences."

Write for websites or publications that match your audience's specific interests your results will prove to be more useful than blasting out a series of mediocre articles on as many sites as you can find.

Hold your head high, be diligent about upholding your standards, and build your trustworthiness in a consistent, steady manner. Don't be tempted to listen to anyone who tells you to "go hard and work your butt off," writing as much content as you can as fast as you can. I have been there and done that as have many of my colleagues, and they will all tell you that's a great way to burn yourself out and get sick of writing very fast.

Write for the audience you know well and devote your energy to doing an outstanding job for these people. They are the ones you know want your stuff, and they will appreciate it – and so will Google and other search engines, because your visitors' time on page will increase, as may your rankings, and so will your conversion rates!

It's much better to start slow and steady and deliver immense value. Build a bond with your prospects.

1.   Use your customer research.

2.   Think in headlines.

3.   Teach and answer questions.

4.   Chunk it down to easily readable bites.

5.   Don't put too much pressure on yourself.

Note: I do understand that some of you will be writing for clients and that you may be wondering how this all fits with a business model based on pushing out a ton of content in a short time. From my experience and others that follow the quality over quantity principle, their articles convert better into extended visits onsite and higher sales, so the value of the person writing the content increases.

Content writers with high conversion rates are hard to find and highly sought after.

If you write posts that do more than create interest, but also build desire and deal with all the obstacles that a website would have to overcome, it makes sense that you will be preconditioning visitors before they arrive on a site. The website owner/webmaster will have less work to do to convert readers once they arrive on their website. Referrals from useful articles and relevant traffic mean bounce rates go down & conversion rates often go up.

Tip: If I need to write a lot of content or recycle general material into many subtopics, I use a tool called SpinRewriter. It is a spinning tool, and it surprises some people that I would use something like this. Its paragraph addition tool is excellent for coming up with the base of a blog post, or for social media posts. They also have a blog syndication service. Check out Spin Rewriter here: https:/// spinrewriter

So here is a summary of the general rules I follow when writing any online content. These principles also apply to print media, but for the benefit of the majority of readers who will be writing for websites, let us assume I am talking about online content.

Mia's top tips for online content writing:

1. Start by doing thorough homework. Spend plenty of time researching your audience: what are they talking about, what are their most significant wants, fears, and concerns, and where they are talking about them online. E.g., reviews, forums, social media, etc.

2. Connect desires with the benefits of your products and services. When I say wishes, I don't just mean desiring a new "widget," I mean, what satisfaction will that widget deliver and how will it make them FEEL. Please list all the positive things they might feel after purchasing it or signing up for it.

3. Don't be afraid to admit weakness and past failures as long as you explain the benefits of those failures and what you learned from them. Remember that making a damaging admission tells your audience you are happy to admit you are not perfect but have learned from your mistakes, and so can they. It also infers that you are

transparent and not trying to hide anything.

4. Talk about your readers' concerns openly and honestly. Validate their reasons for having those concerns and then help them get past them through your processes.

5. Help your readers, serve them, give them something of value to make them feel positive about and more confident in what you have to offer. Demonstrate what you can do for them in small steps.

6. Bond with readers and show them you are serious about helping them. Align yourself with them by talking about situations you've been in that they might relate to, and share how you have overcome things they might fear, but that they think they will have to overcome to get what they want.

7. Clearly explain the value of your products or services to appeal to their logical brain. People are emotional beings, but when it comes to handing over cash - they switch into a pragmatic mode. At this point, they will be looking for reasons to justify buying something. They also want to feel like they deserve it, so give them an excuse and a

justification to feel good about purchasing this over something else for which they could spend their money.

8. Add social proof such as examples of how the products or services have helped someone else, and case studies or quotes by third-party sources noting the benefits of your products or services.

9. Namedrop sources of authority and any publications they have released about stats or topics that relate to what you are selling. Grow your credibility by showing you've done your homework and are citing facts rather than throwing in a whole lot of words to try and sound official.

10. Explain what your reader can expect if they do what you ask them to do. Please give your audience a clear outline of what's likely to be required of them (e.g., sign up, register, free trial). Tell them what they can expect when they click on a link and make sure what you promised is delivered at the destination you are sending them to.

Use the same wording on any buttons and links your readers are going to see when they arrive at the site you are sending them to.

In other words, don't make them work for or guess what to do as the next step.

11. Create a clear and concise call to action that is explanatory e.g., *to get that do this now or before [insert time limit or number limit]*.

12. Add a summary, P.S., or reminder outlining what your readers can expect when they follow your call to action.

13. Remember, you can also use your copy to stay in touch with your audience by offering an invitation to join your newsletter or invite people to follow you on social media.

That's pretty much it. That's my checklist when writing content. I like to ensure that all the articles I produce contain these elements. If I miss anything, I can generally expect to see it reflected in lower conversion rates.

Following these principles makes for satisfying reading for your audience. They will feel like they have had a comprehensive experience, and you'll be preconditioning them when they reach their destination because you will have done much of the work to warm them up to a purchase. You will have given them something that genuinely helps them get closer to their goal.

Don't try to be perfect, it's more important to think of your content like a conversation with a new friend. If you have relayed back to a person how they feel about something, and are positive, helpful, or useful, you will both feel good.

So have fun writing. Have an awesome day, and I wish you all the best in your writing endeavors.

Recommended Tools

Research Tools

Keyword Atlas - keyword research tool (Youtube, Amazon, Google etc)

Content Samurai Keyword Research Tool (Google) https://www.contentsamurai.com/c/eziseo-cs-freetrial

Favorite Marketing Books – Must Reads

The Adweek Copywriting Handbook: The Ultimate Guide to Writing Powerful Advertising and Marketing Copy from One of America's Top Copywriters – Joe Sugarman

Almost Alchemy: Make Any Business Of Any Size Produce More With Fewer And Less – Dan S. Kennedy

Triggers: 30 Sales Tools You Can Use to Control the Mind of Your Prospect to Motivate, Influence, and Persuade – Joe Sugarman

No B.S. Time Management for Entrepreneurs: The Ultimate No Holds Barred Kick Butt Take No Prisoners

Guide to Time Productivity and Sanity – Dan Kennedy

Influence: Science and Practice (5th Edition) – Robert B. Cialdini

Contagious: Why Things Catch On – Jonah Berger

www.ingramcontent.com/pod-product-compliance
Lightning Source LLC
Chambersburg PA
CBHW061435180526
45170CB00004B/1420